"More than just a book about crowdfunding, this is a valuable contribution to the debate about democratizing the economy. Accessible and thought-provoking, it puts questions of power and control over money where they belong – at the heart of the analysis."

Christine Berry, author and Director of IPPR North

"Change which gives all humans dignity doesn't come from words alone, but from institutions that give life to our collective needs and strengths. We can only finance the future we want if financial systems themselves honour a more equal, democratic and sustainable society. This incredible and timely book shows us how."

Neal Lawson, author and Director of Compass

MARK DAVIS AND BRUCE DAVIS

CROWDFUNDING AND THE DEMOCRATIZATION OF FINANCE

BRISTOL
UNIVERSITY
PRESS

First published in Great Britain in 2022 by

Bristol University Press
University of Bristol
1–9 Old Park Hill
Bristol
BS2 8BB
UK
t: +44 (0)117 954 5940
e: bup-info@bristol.ac.uk

Details of international sales and distribution partners are available at
bristoluniversitypress.co.uk

© Bristol University Press 2022

British Library Cataloguing in Publication Data
A catalogue record for this book is available from the British Library

ISBN 978-1-5292-1673-8 hardcover
ISBN 978-1-5292-1674-5 ePub
ISBN 978-1-5292-1675-2 ePdf

Cover design: Bristol University Press
Front cover image: Jim Le Fevre

For Zygmunt
who started it all

Contents

About the Authors

Mark Davis is Associate Professor of Sociology at the University of Leeds, UK, where he founded the Bauman Institute in 2010. Supported by grants from the European Commission (EC) and UK Research and Innovation (UKRI), Mark's work argues that social relations shape how we spend, borrow, save and invest, with implications for policy and practice. To date, his research has improved investor protection in UK crowdfunding markets; developed new prosumer business models and innovative finance options for Europe's green energy transition; and, with Abundance, co-created Community Municipal Investments (CMIs) to help finance local net zero projects. Mark is an expert evaluator for the EC's Marie Skłodowska-Curie Actions programme, a member of Friends Provident Foundation's programme advisory group, and sits on the Editorial Board of the British Sociological Association's journal, *Sociology*.

Bruce Davis is Co-founder and Joint Managing Director of Abundance Investment, the world's first regulated investment-based crowdfunding platform, which is focused on green and social investments. Bruce has worked as an ethnographic researcher and consultant to a number of financial services companies and was part of the creative team behind the launch of the first peer-to-peer (P2P) lending service, Zopa. Bruce has also been involved in the development of a number of important regulatory and legislative innovations to support crowdfunding, including the Innovative Finance ISA (IFISA). He is a member of the UK Government's Green Finance Taskforce, a founding director of the UK Crowdfunding Association (UKCFA), a senior fellow of the Finance Innovation Lab and Visiting Research Fellow at the Bauman Institute, University of Leeds, UK.

★★★

Since we are asked this question a lot, allow us to confirm for the reader at the outset that we are not related.

Acknowledgements

This book is the outcome of a long conversation that first began in a church hall in Hay-on-Wye on Sunday 24 May 2009. That afternoon, Bruce was in the audience to hear the world-renowned sociologist Zygmunt Bauman speak to the topic of 'The Tyranny of Freedom', part of the HowtheLightGetsIn Festival hosted by the Institute of Ideas (IAI). With his wife Janina having fallen ill, and fresh from their recent discussions about the possibility of founding a Bauman Institute at the University of Leeds, Zygmunt asked Mark to honour the obligation instead by delivering a lecture in his absence. To the great credit of the people who gathered inside a baking hot church hall that afternoon, they hid their disappointment well as Mark stepped up to the lectern. In the post-event milieu, Bruce introduced himself and we began our long conversation about freedom, consumerism, choice and alternatives to the mainstream financial system.

Those alternatives are what had encouraged Bruce to travel so far to hear Zygmunt speak, having been inspired by Bauman's account of 'liquid modernity'. Bauman's description was of a world where once 'solid' institutions, lifestyles and social norms were being rapidly dissolved into 'liquid' by the turbulence caused to nation states via the suddenly extra-territorial flows of global capital. This was creating a 'liquid world' where people were increasingly abandoned to their own individual wit and muscle to find strategies of survival. In the uncertainty and insecurity that followed, power was gradually separated from politics with divorce proceedings apparently pending. If the global flows of mainstream finance had fully captured the power of mainstream politics, then the challenge of creating alternatives to both in a way that harnessed the new opportunities of internet-enabled connectivity was taken up by a first wave of financial innovators. It became part of Bruce's own journey to understand 'the social life of money'. This formed the basis of his day job consulting with financial services companies and underpinned the development of the idea of P2P lending. Bruce had been asked by the 'FinTech' visionary, Richard Duvall, to join a group of finance professionals that became known as the New Barn Collective. This group, which met regularly to discuss ideas and to collaborate on projects in Richard's new barn (the clue was in the name) was the catalyst for the creation of this financial revolution.

Like Zygmunt, Richard was a man of infectious energy, vision and chutzpah. Instead of living to the grand age of 91, however, Richard's life was tragically cut short by cancer at just 44, a few years after the successful launch of Zopa. Following a brief interlude to develop a new brand of whisky (Monkey Shoulder) in 2008, Bruce was then introduced to green entrepreneur, Karl Harder, by a mutual friend, the sociologist William Davies. They met to discuss how to revolutionize green finance over a coffee in the British Library, while Karl was working on his MBA course. The concept for the Abundance platform was born.

Abundance only became a reality following a long struggle against the bureaucracy of the regulator, who had never had to authorize something completely new before. Its approval owed particular thanks to the hard work and stubborn resilience of the third Abundance co-founder, Louise Wilson.

Over the next ten years, Abundance would develop a number of 'firsts'. These include the co-creation of a new category of crowdfunding product, the CMI – essentially, a form of local government green bond – that was developed in partnership with Mark and his research team at the University of Leeds. Launched in the UK on 16 July 2020, CMIs are now enabling councils to raise stable, low risk finance direct from their residents in order to deliver local net zero projects.

Back in Hay-on-Wye on that busy summer afternoon in 2009, we never imagined we would end up writing a book together, still less during such an unsettling and unstable time as the COVID-19 pandemic. We are thus especially grateful for the support and encouragement of some truly wonderful people without whom we could not have written the book. Begging the indulgence of the reader, we'd like to take some time to acknowledge them.

First, we both extend our thanks to the team at Bristol University Press who first saw merit in the project. In particular, our senior commissioning editor, Paul Stevens, has been a great champion of the book and helped to improve the project significantly. To our four anonymous reviewers, our sincere thanks for your immensely helpful comments on the original proposal. To our final reviewer of the full manuscript, thank you for showing such faith in the book. We're grateful also to Tamsin Ballard, Emma Cook, Annie Rose and Ruth Wallace who ably guided us through the production process and were open to Jim Le Fevre's creative suggestions for the front cover. Thanks also to Bahar Celik Muller for working hard to ensure the book finds its audience.

Mark wishes to thank his colleagues at Leeds for taking an interest in the project and offering their encouragement. My thanks in particular to: Kim Allen, Andrew Brown, Donal Brown, Tom Campbell, Laura Cartwright, Paul Chatterton, Claudia Coveney, Gary Dymski, Daniel Edmiston, Andy Gouldson, Joanne Greenhalgh, Steve Hall, Margo Hanson, Ruth Holliday, Greg Hollin, Sarah Irwin, Glenn McCauley, Lucie Middlemiss, Simon Moore, Rachel Muers, Alice Owen, Anne Owen, Jack Palmer, Katy Roelich, Robert Thornton-Lee, Matthew Treherne and Katy Wright. Steve Hall and Donal Brown keep me going with a friendship beyond value. Steve's comments on the first draft – unpublishable here – improved the book immeasurably and I'm grateful for his critical insight and honest wit. Further afield, I have benefited enormously from conversations with: Tim Braunholtz-Speight, Anna Fielding, Arthur Hirsch, Lars Holstenkamp, Leigh-Claire La Berge, Matilde Massó Lago, Kristian Petrick, Nick Robins, Katy Shaw, Robert Wardrop and Julia Wittmayer. Closer to home, life during the pandemic has once again revealed the immense fortune of friends and family. My heartfelt thanks go to you all. Most importantly, none of this would have been possible without the love, support and endless impatience for the next adventure of my own little family – the 'Zoo', Ziggy and Kimba, and my wife Kathryn. I owe it all to you Fisky.

Bruce wishes to thank his partner Lara, for putting up with his 'middle of the night' chapter inspirations, his children, Effie, Phoebe, Cameron, Eva and Mamie, for reminding me why it matters that finance works for a better world, my colleagues at Abundance especially Karl and Louise, my long-time public relations adviser and friend Martin Campbell for his unfailing support and insights, and Sophy Fearnley-Whittingstall for reminding me of the benefits of a journalist's brevity. Thanks also to Zoe Williams, who would rarely let me pay for lunch and whose conversations have helped to shape many of the ideas in this book.

Preface

Do you know where your money is? If you read 'money' and immediately think of cash, then there's a very fair chance that you've just pictured notes and coins in a purse or a wallet, or perhaps imagined a big steel vault in a heavily secured basement room in a bank. Either way, you've likely sought to reassure yourself that your money is safe. But if you read 'money' and instead thought of digital numbers on a smartphone screen, or more imaginatively still, considered your pension, savings and investments, then there's an equally good chance that you don't know exactly where your money is at all. And this suggests a far more fundamental question. If you don't know where your money is, then how do you know what your money is *doing*?

While most people feel supremely confident that they know precisely what money is, and what they would choose to do should they suddenly have more of it, they are equally uncertain and anxious when it comes to the seemingly more complex matters of finance. At least a part of the problem here is that we tend to use these two terms interchangeably and in different contexts, often misunderstanding their meaning because of it. This is not just a problem for everyday conversations – it creates problems for those of us who study it and who seek to make sense of the way that we think about and use money, and the ways in which financial systems are developed around money.

Throughout this book, our study investigates the stories and myths about money that have led to the creation of different systems of finance, from the *eranos* loans of ancient Greece to the FinTech and Crypto revolutions of the early 21st century. In so doing, we suggest that finance has not always been the preserve of the elite professional, but is rather something that develops in different ways, bound by time and cultures, and often alters as a response to crisis. The shape of finance at any given moment in history and across cultures, then, depends upon the social relations and moral values that hold those societies together. Far from being formal and rational, finance is a vital, messy and evolving part of social life, providing the means through which money is used to negotiate and create spectacular outcomes – but which today is being utilized almost exclusively for private gain rather than the delivery of social, political and environmental public goods.

Our argument starts from the principle that how and where we decide to spend, borrow, save and invest makes a material difference to the type of world that we are creating for ourselves and for future generations. What we do with our money really matters. If we want a radically better world to the one we currently inhabit – and if we want that world to be fairer, more equitable and more sustainable – then we are going to have to do radically different things with our money. And yet, as our opening questions illustrate, we often don't know precisely where our money is or what it is doing. Thanks to the way that money flows somewhat invisibly around our globally connected societies, we typically have precious little say in what sorts of material outcomes our decisions about money are driving. Indeed, the destination of money is largely dictated by just a small handful of mainstream financial institutions to whom we habitually give power and control over our money.

Enter crowdfunding. The idea of coming together to fund projects and businesses has already motivated people to have their say and to move their money in support of delivering such diverse outcomes as church hall renovations, a utility-scale solar park, wind turbines, personal loans for home improvements, small business lending, support for social enterprises and local councils, social housing, the repurposing of public land and buildings for community use, and the next big thing in craft beer. Returns for investors range from the payment of financial interest to the generation of green energy and rebuilding the social fabric of a community.

Our purpose in this book is to put forward an argument that crowdfunding, which we argue is actually a 2,500-year-old new idea, can begin to put the power and control over our money back into the hands of people. Today's digitally enabled form of crowdfunding represents the latest stage of a shifting relationship between democracy and finance that throughout human history – from the ancient city-state of Athens right up to the COVID-19 pandemic – has been renegotiated and resettled following periods of crisis. In presenting the reader with a pre-history of crowdfunding, we argue that crisis has always been an important catalyst for the development of different models of democratic societies and that the present moment requires a similar response. Along the way, we will show that finance plays a key role in the health of our democracies but that it urgently needs to rediscover its sense of purpose as a servant of society if it is to help overcome, rather than exacerbate, the grand challenges of the 21st century. By exploding the myths and stories about money that continue to cloud how we understand and make use of this vital tool of social transformation, we turn not to mainstream economics but to the different sociological and anthropological accounts of money to help us take what money actually 'does' more seriously. In this way, we want to rethink who gets to make decisions about what we use money for and who should hold power over what we can do with the change in our pockets.

Our research and professional practice to date have demonstrated to us that crowdfunding has the potential to disrupt the incumbent power of large banks and mainstream financial institutions, while simultaneously enhancing the potential of individuals to participate in delivering 'real-world' outcomes by moving their money into new financial channels that transparently deliver better environmental and social outcomes. We believe there is a genuine opportunity here for new forms of civic engagement that may also augment local and national democratic processes as people become more socially and financially invested in improving the well-being of their communities. More ambitious still, we argue that crowdfunding and P2P finance has the radical potential to redefine the relationship between the market and the state by changing the balance of power between finance and democracy.

Confronted with the need to build a fairer, greener recovery from the global shock of the COVID-19 pandemic, and to address those systemic and intersectional inequalities that it has amplified, the decision to choose a more democratic finance seems to us truly urgent. After all, if it is not to help provision the things that the planet and our societies need, then what is finance for? How can we better hold it to account? Is there a way of changing the destination of money in such a way that delivers better outcomes for people and planet, and not only more profit for shareholders? And, what is the role for crowdfunding in democratizing finance?

Answering these questions fully is a huge task beyond the scope of this book. But what we can do in the pages that follow is to show how innovations in crowdfunding and other alternative forms of financial practice get us closer to a more democratic finance. By being founded upon different understandings of money, we argue they are able to point the way ahead to a more stable and just financial system where we all get the chance to benefit. We aim to provoke a public debate about the relationship between democracy and finance, to show how moments of crisis in human history have often led to a renewed settlement between them, and how crowdfunding offers a viable structure for challenging the dominance of mainstream finance.

Structure of the book

Both authors have been closely involved in and engaged with the UK crowdfunding sector since its inception, as an academic and a practitioner. We are therefore well-placed to offer a blend of insider and outsider perspectives on the potential and the problems of crowdfunding. In the chapters that follow, we offer an interpretation of crowdfunding as a form of democratic finance as viewed from these two positions.

Chapter One sets the scene of the present crisis of finance and lays the foundations for how we are using the idea of democracy throughout the book. We introduce three models of democracy to reveal important criteria for assessing crowdfunding as a form of democratic finance, and begin to explore who really controls your money.

Chapter Two introduces the reader to the basics of crowdfunding, the types of models that exist and what each of them means for your money. We briefly survey the size and scale of global crowdfunding sectors, before returning to the UK where both authors are based to hear from crowdfunding platforms themselves about their role in democratizing finance.

Chapter Three traces the history of crowdfunding back to ancient Athens, offering insights into the relationship between the birth of democracy and finance, including how moments of crisis have led to the renewal of both. Here, we also examine how our beliefs about money, and our readiness to trust other people with it, are rooted in a constant interplay between individual self-reliance and shared social responsibilities that plays a role in politics as much in ancient Athens as it does today.

Chapter Four reflects upon all of these issues by raising the importance of the destination of money. We are less concerned with the relatively abstract study of what money is, and draw instead upon ideas from sociology and anthropology to point to the significance of understanding what money does. We show how these insights help to form the basis of a more democratic and ultimately sustainable financial system, which we see embodied in the principles and practices of crowdfunding.

Chapter Five extends our argument by reflecting on the potential futures of crowdfunding and the democratization of finance. We explore the paradox of financial inclusion; the idea of investment as a social act surrounded by long-standing taboos; and, how mainstream finance today is far more interested in managing the existing wealth of the rich than in creating it for the poorer members of society. Since there are also those who read the innovations of Bitcoin and other cryptocurrencies and cryptoassets through the lens of democratic finance, we show how this market is driven by a very different worldview to the one we see embodied in crowdfunding.

Finally, we close the book by bringing the various threads of our argument together, assessing crowdfunding against our three models of democracy outlined in Chapter One, and invite the reader to reflect upon their own understanding and use of money in the hope they may recognize the change in their pocket and act to alter its destination.

In the hope of being helpful to the reader, we have chosen not to interrupt the flow of our narrative with frequent citations on the page itself, instead providing notes and a list of references at the end of the book. As this will show, we rely throughout on a number of other thinkers, as well as drawing upon evidence from our professional lives. Inevitably, some who read this book will recognize their own contribution to our argument. Proceeding in this way, any errors of interpretation are entirely our own and the solutions we propose will likely differ to those advocated by others.

Finally, we hope the following pages are a welcome contribution to rediscovering money as a form of mutual trust and as the most powerful tool of social transformation ever devised by human societies. We hope also that the story of crowdfunding we tell will serve to embolden those who, like us, seek to build a radically more democratic financial system to the one we have today.

Mark Davis and Bruce Davis
September 2021

ONE

The Crisis of Finance

In a still more profound way than we may think, we are in a period of crisis. Every aspect of the human condition and the social institutions we have made together are today in doubt. In the popular imagination, a crisis is a marker of something vexing that is to be overcome. It enjoys a temporal dimension, seeming to diagnose a present problem at the same time as it already imagines a future moment when the crisis will cease to be, when things will 'return to normal'. Writing this book together during the the COVID-19 pandemic that began in 2020, that desire for a return to normal life is especially acute, currently providing the basis for a new and common hope all around the world.

And yet, the extent to which we should want to 'return' to what we previously understood as 'normal' is immediately problematic. The 21st century has already seen an unprecedented cadence of social, environmental, political and economic emergencies that have called into question the belief systems that have hitherto underpinned that normality. These emergencies have resulted in a steady decline in our trust in the value of our democratic political systems, which is seldom attributed to a globalized financial system that is too often responsible for driving these outcomes. The COVID-19 pandemic is providing humanity with an opportunity for a 'great reset' with the chance to 'build back better', but some are asking if we really want a swift return to the way things were. Instead, should we be choosing something better, a new way of organizing social life such that we can respond to the challenges of today and tomorrow, not yesterday? After all, we learn from Janet Roitman that if everything is in 'crisis' then perhaps nothing is.[1] Is our state of perpetual crisis itself just the 'new normal'? Suddenly emptied of its popular meaning then, how can we be in a period of crisis?

Reflecting on the events of 2008, when the world was first hit by those shockwaves of the global crash that still reverberate today, Sylvia Walby argues that '[f]inance caused the crisis. More precisely, the failure of the state to regulate finance caused the crisis. Finance is intrinsically unstable; but this can be mitigated. The reduction in democratic control over finance led to the financial crisis'.[2] Given the urgent need to tackle the global Climate Emergency,[3] to overcome the democratic deficit[4] and to correct ever-widening inequalities,[5] the case for radical democratic reform of the global financial system appears to be increasingly pressing.

Returning to Roitman, the root of the word 'crisis' (from the ancient Greek word *krinô*, meaning to choose, decide, or judge) means that we are being compelled to make a profound decision, a judgement between alternative futures. In a term deployed by the sociologist Zygmunt Bauman[6] – to whom this book is dedicated – we thus find ourselves in an *interregnum*. This idea was originally employed to mark that period of acute uncertainty that was felt throughout a society during the constitutional 'gap' created by the transition from one sovereign ruler to the next.

Bauman reimagines the original concept of interregnum in such a way that it goes far beyond the routine process of transferring hereditary power. Instead, Bauman finds it sociologically useful for helping to capture those profound moments when an entire social order starts to fragment and to lose its authority, but unnervingly at a time when there is no new social order currently ready to take its place. The Italian philosopher Antonio Gramsci had earlier expressed the same idea: 'The crisis consists precisely in the fact that the old is dying and the new cannot be born; in this interregnum a great variety of morbid symptoms appear.'[7]

In moments of crisis, then, the realities of our existence are laid bare, and we are forced to make a decision. Do we find a way out of the present impasse caused by this societal interregnum by choosing to return to the 'old Ruler', to the ideas and institutions upon which we had previously felt life was good, secure and made sense? In his last book, published posthumously, Bauman labelled this particular instinct 'retrotopic', a desire to 'go back' to how society used to be before the world somehow became uncontrollable and so incomprehensible.[8] It is this instinct that encouraged millions to choose to 'take *back* control' and to make ourselves 'great *again*'. Retrotopia is an impulse to turn away from the future and instead rehearse the past, and is as common today on the popular Left as it is on the popular Right of politics.[9]

Surprisingly, this analysis of the crisis is found not only among sociologists and philosophers, but also in the exalted pages of the *Financial Times*. On 6 July 2020, the newspaper's associate editor and chief economics editor, Martin Wolf, argued that the world has experienced two interregnums since the Second World War.[10] The first was the period of high inflation during the 1970s, which was the crisis that led to a new settlement between democracy and finance in what Wolf calls the 'Thatcher-Reagan consensus'. The second of those interregnums was triggered by the global financial crisis of 2008 and has endured to the present day, when the global health crisis of COVID-19 is demanding another new settlement. Noting that anger and despair at the financial system has played its part in the rise of populist nationalism throughout Western societies, Wolf argues that we must rediscover a sense of citizenship based on loyalty to democracy, concern that all should live a fulfilled life, and the creation of an economy that allows all citizens to flourish.

This book is focused on the possibilities for creating just such an economy. As democratic citizens, we need to get a tight hold of the institutions of mainstream finance, understand them better and find out how their current organizational structures drive negative outcomes in our lives. Having done so, we then need to build new ones that don't. We need to force finance out of the shadows in order to see how its interests sit behind many of the unfair and seemingly inexplicable decisions of national and local governments, as well as private and public companies. We need to grasp that there is no natural law of economics that refuses the greater participation of everyone in finance. We need to find ways of building collective confidence in saying to finance that our communities need to build this or that public infrastructure to make our lives better and more harmonious with the environment, and then together move our money in ways that ensure those things actually get built. This is a far safer and surer strategy to provision the things we all need for a flourishing and fulfilled life than continuing to leave those decisions to the faceless denizens of distant glass towers, with little more than a faint hope that the beneficent light of global capital will reflect our way to one day shine upon us.

A vital first step in the creation of a citizen-led economy is to see money differently in order to change what it does. At the moment, money is doing precious little for the many, and far too much for the few. Changing what money does means altering its purpose and this first requires a fundamental change of mindset, a revolution in the head. After all, the purpose of money is not set in stone for all time. Lots of different objects – from sheaths of barley and Kula shells through to paper notes and metal coins – have all counted as money at different stages of history. Money is a social construct, a mutual system of trust created in the human imagination and represented by whatever we choose to call 'money' in order to negotiate and organize complex social relationships. As the economist Paul G. Fisher, former member of the Bank of England and now academic, outlines with commendable insight: 'The rules of economic conduct and economics as a field of enquiry are not immutable natural laws. They are a set of tools which generate a shared, imagined mental construct which changes over time, and indeed can be changed as we so please.'[11]

Put simply, we argue against acquiescing to the vainglorious return of any 'old Ruler' to the throne. To insist upon a single, charismatic leader – embodied by a single individual or a single dominant sector – goes against the principles of democracy and portends a darker political future ahead. Instead, we suggest that the crisis of finance today requires us to take a risk by assuming our collective responsibility as citizens of democracy for repurposing money in the interests of people and planet. In making our case for crowdfunding as one of the structures capable of delivering a more democratic finance, this book is about giving each of us the confidence to take that risk and to embrace the truth that there are no immutable or natural economic laws. Crowdfunding provides us with one way to decide collectively upon what we want the financial system to look like.

Before we come to make our case for crowdfunding, however, let us first begin to force finance out of the shadows.

The financial Leviathan

So who was the 'old Ruler'? Since 2004, during which the world has endured major financial, environmental and global health emergencies, the number of billionaires has quadrupled and their combined wealth has risen to just short of US$8 trillion.[12] At the same time, the finance industry – namely the people that we knowingly or unwittingly entrust with our money, empowering them to make investment decisions on our behalf – has increased its assets under management (AUM)[13] from US$37 trillion to an estimated US$111 trillion in 2020.[14] This represents almost 40 per cent of the total financial assets of pension funds, sovereign wealth funds, High Net Worth individuals and so-called 'Mass Affluent' individuals in the world.

Collectively, these groups are estimated to own around US$280 trillion of assets. Of these companies, whose revenues from this global industry are estimated to be more than US$650 billion annually, just the top 20 firms now control more than 43 per cent of those AUM.[15] What these figures show is that we have created a Leviathan of finance that controls most of what people typically understand as being 'the money in the world'. It is they who control it and decide upon its destination, choosing which sectors to invest in, which industries are 'safe', and which geographies 'deserve' to receive investment. Just like Hobbes's reinterpretation of the mythical sea creature, this financial Leviathan appears also to have been granted the absolute power of a sovereign ruler, despite the democratic structures that are supposed to hold it in check.

The present crisis forces a decision. Do we give our consent to be governed by this 'old Ruler', or do we decide if its inability to guarantee peace and security for people and planet is a terminal breach of the social contract? Indeed, it is precisely because finance behaves like a capricious sovereign power, seemingly disinterested in the consequences of its actions on the lives of people and planet, that people reasonably conclude it to be an external and malevolent force that simply happens to people. Why choose the Leviathan if it helps to instigate a 'war of all against all' rather than to prevent it? Finance, a human-made system that is created and sustained through a series of myths and stories about money that guide how we engage with it, therefore needs what all hostile rulers eventually face: a revolution in both thought and practice.

We argue that crowdfunding offers one way to instigate this revolution and, as we will see in Chapter Two, represents a decentralized and somewhat anarchic response to the idea of a single 'sovereign' ruler. Rather than simply replacing one illegitimate Leviathan with another 'more legitimate' one, crowdfunding as a sector seeks to decentralize control to the 'crowd' through the use of online platforms enabling a silent negotiation of preferences over investment to emerge. As with previous attempts to escape the tyranny of monarchical rule, the solution resides in giving more power to the people.

It is common to characterize such epochal shifts in power and control over our money as 'financialization', a shorthand for social processes that have created the global institutions, legal frameworks, regulations and beliefs that make up the mainstream finance industry.[16] An important part of these processes is finance's increasing 'professionalization', having become the preserve of a particular power-knowledge elite in the last four decades especially. The idea that 'finance' should only inhabit the formal, rarefied spaces of professional financiers has emerged as a result of the gradual impoverishment of our collective public understanding of money, aided by the deliberate strengthening and solidifying of the myths and stories we place around money. In other words, it serves the interests of a privileged few rather than the public many to perpetuate myths about money that, as we will show, have long since been discredited.

In effect, it is the enduring myths about money that enable the creation of a finance system akin to a 'gilded cage' into which we have hitherto decided to entrust all of our individual and collective hopes for future prosperity. These myths about money, aided and abetted by a financial system that seeks to perpetuate them as a mechanism of its own self-reproduction, are limiting our collective imagination to dethrone our 'old Ruler' by democratizing finance.

Why 'democratic finance'?

The year 2004 was also significant for another reason. This was the year that marked the creation of a new form of finance. More accurately, it saw the 'rebirth' of a form of finance that so far has cumulatively led to tens of billions of dollars being mobilized through a radically different form of investment to those provided by mainstream financial institutions. This is what we call crowdfunding and its sister sector P2P finance. The founding principles of this 'new' way of investing money are diametrically opposed to those of the mainstream finance industry. Currently active in more than 180 countries around the world,[17] crowdfunding and P2P finance continue to provide hard evidence of a rebuttal to those who succumb to what Zygmunt Bauman laments as the 'TINA Syndrome',[18] a tendency too hastily to proclaim that 'there is no alternative', in this case to the power and dominance of mainstream finance.

Indeed, while the largesse of billionaires may attract the public's attention, and their ire, for sitting aboard their yachts and private jets as they travel to and from their tax haven island paradises, or for embarking upon their personal space crusades, two simultaneous and opposing insurgencies have been underway that have received far less attention from either the media commentariat or the wider public. The first insurgency is the rapid growth of the asset management industry, which has seen the wholesale transfer of control over our collective investible/financial assets to a class of professional financiers who can now make or break the decisions of democratically mandated governments and their citizens by hoarding the power to invest for their future.

The second, very different, insurgency has seen an explosion in new and innovative forms of local, community and P2P finance that have started to challenge the power and dominance of mainstream finance, unleashing a new wave of citizen-led finance reborn for the internet age. This second insurgency has created new ways of funding everything from high-tech start-ups through to green energy infrastructure, from renovating disused public land to make it suitable for community use through to covering the costs of legal fees for those financially excluded from pursuing justice. This second insurgency has given millions of people the confidence to make their own small investment decisions and to change the destination of their money.

And though currently short of a full-blown democratic revolution in finance, this second insurgency shouldn't be underestimated, as the power held by millions of citizens collectively to make different decisions about their money represents a significant threat to the status quo. In early 2021, for example, the financial Leviathan's leading 'shock troops', the hedge funds, found themselves in a pitched battle on the markets of Wall Street as millions of small (and not so small) investors made a decision to act collectively. Fed up with the predatory hedge fund practice of short selling[19] against companies, a war broke out over the shares of the US-based electronics and gaming merchandise retailer, GameStop. With the hedge funds betting that the stock in the company would drop, millions of small investors began buying up small stocks in the company through a practice known as short squeezing[20] that drove the stock price of GameStop skywards within a matter of days. While the outcomes of this event are not fully understood at the time of writing, what's fascinating is how people decided to frame this particular event in terms of the democratization of finance, suddenly realizing how ordinary small investors were entirely capable of challenging the values and practices of those professional elites that not only control our financial assets, but who also increasingly hold power over the decisions of those remaining public professionals who would control our money. Of course, as with any revolution, the old Ruler can be relied upon to fight back.[21]

These repeated calls for the democratization of finance – whether of the stock markets of Wall Street or investments in the tech start-up companies of London's Silicon Roundabout – reflect how the history of democracy and finance are intimately entwined. As we will see in Chapter Three, we find examples of how public recognition both of the extremes of financial inequalities and how the financial system's behaviour helps to perpetuate those extremes subsequently leads to the desire to break up the power of financial institutions. Such moments of crisis have often led to forms of democratic renewal, something we insist is urgently needed today.

As we write in the spring of 2021, the newly elected president of the United States, Joe Biden, has cited the threat to democracy as one of his top priorities.[22] At the same time, an ex-central banker, 'Super Mario' Draghi, was recently installed as Italian prime minister. Draghi has been invited to form a government in order to marshal the country through its economic recovery from the pandemic without recourse to a popular mandate.[23] Twenty-four years ago, the UK's Chancellor of the Exchequer, Labour's Gordon Brown, started what is now a global trend by taking the decision to make the Bank of England the wholly independent controller and regulator of the UK monetary and financial system. Brown's professed motive was to end the economic 'boom and bust' cycles by ensuring the UK, and perhaps the wider world, would no longer suffer the consequences of politically motivated financial crises. Today, at the apex of this line of thinking, we have the spectacle of an ex-central banker being seen as the only suitable candidate to be the *de facto* independent controller of a democratic political system in crisis. Time need not be wasted in asking the citizens of Italy's democracy for their view; the only blessing that matters it seems is that swiftly given by the global bond markets.

In this and countless other ways, our democracies are in danger of giving up control over money, and so also the investment decisions that directly shape our world, to a professionalized group of financiers with barely a comment and certainly without much of a fight. One thing we can agree upon about money is that trust is fundamental. As we outline in Chapter Four, sociologists and anthropologists see money as fundamentally a system of social trust. The finance system is built and relies upon that trust. How curious, then, that when it comes to decisions about money, we seem unwilling to trust ourselves. Instead, we prefer to hand decision-making power over the well-being of people and planet to a class of financial technocrats who are themselves often mistrustful of democracy and the financial motives and competencies of the citizens it represents.

This book deliberately provides a route to trusting ourselves with money. It aims to (re)build our confidence by providing an alternative account of our current financial system and by looking at how we can empower citizens to take control of their money. Only in this way can we start to redirect its flow in order to deliver more socially and environmentally positive outcomes. Instead of seeking to understand crowdfunding and P2P finance as marginal players within a mainstream financial system, and so measuring its success only in terms of investment size and volume, we trace their development back through history to an understanding of the 'social life of money' that has existed since ancient times. In this way, we examine how its latest incarnation is of profound importance to a world seeking to dethrone the financial Leviathan.

Models of democracy

In seeking that dethronement and arguing for a more democratic finance, it is clearly important to be clear which models of democracy we are drawing upon. Democracy exists on a spectrum from a relatively narrow focus upon the rights of citizens to vote in formal elections, through participatory models that seek to enhance the levels of citizen involvement in decision-making processes, and on to more radical and conflict-based practices. Different models of democracy reflect various perspectives on the purpose of democracy too, with significant changes to eligibility since its inception in ancient Athens. The right to democratic participation can often somewhat mirror the right to access finance too, especially if we consider the historical exclusion of women. It is shocking to remember that a woman's right to a bank account, so that they might hold their own money independently of their husband or male relative, was only enshrined in law as recently as the 1960s and 1970s in the US and UK respectively. This was a full 80–90 years after France had enacted its law in 1881, initially permitting single women the right to access finance, and subsequently also for married women five years later.[24]

Variations of democratic participation can range from formal membership of political parties or trade unions through to more individualized modes of political engagement, such as exercising consumer choice in the marketplace to select products labelled as 'ethical'. More recently, this 'ethical' choice has been extended beyond shopping habits also to include decisions over how best to engage with financial products and services. One of the aims of this book is to begin to sensitize the reader to their own understanding and use of money in much the same way that a culture of 'ethical consumerism' has managed to sensitize people to how and where they choose to shop. If where we buy is just as important as what we buy, then we propose that *how* we buy also matters. This line of thinking helped to inspire 2020's celebrity-driven *Make My Money Matter* campaign coordinated by the film director Richard Curtis, which drew attention to the fact that decisions about how to invest a pension are 27 times more impactful on the environment than consumer choices to buy green and sustainable products.[25]

What this expanded idea of participation reveals is that democracy is seen frequently to involve far more than just turning up to ballot boxes at irregular intervals or registering for postal votes. Just as people assert their hopes and values by voting as citizens in formal democratic elections, those values can also be expressed through the different ways in which money is invested. Today, democratic participation also includes numerous modes of civic, civil and service-user participation, such as engaging in grassroots activities, volunteering with third sector charities, service providers and non-governmental organizations (NGOs). Civil society is an essential support for democracy, occupying that important space between the market and the state in order, it is hoped, to act as a vital check on the authority of both. In arguing that crowdfunding and P2P finance represent a form of democratic engagement, it is these more expanded forms of civic participation that we hold in mind. Indeed, it was this idea that helped to shape the alternative model of civic finance we created in 2019, which became known as Community Municipal Investments, or CMIs, launched in the UK in late 2020,[26] and pointing to a devolved future shaped as much by principles of municipal socialism as community capitalism.[27] To help frame our argument throughout the book, we next outline three 'ideal-type' models of democracy. These models help us to develop criteria by which to assess how far crowdfunding and P2P finance can be seen as democratizing.[28]

When thinking about democracy, the most familiar idea that comes to mind is what we call the *Representative-Aggregative* model. This is where a formal distance is established between citizens and those who actually govern by making decisions on their behalf. In this model, people choose from a list of candidates that they believe will best represent their interests and whose agenda best aligns with their own values. The model is founded upon the idea that people are primarily self-interested, and so by selecting a professional class of politicians to represent the views of citizens we collectively arrive at the most effective and efficient form of government by aggregation. The failings of this model are also familiar, of course, contributing to increases in apathy among voting citizens around the world, the result of under-representation of disparate views and seemingly too marginal a difference between those candidates we are invited to elect. The distance between citizens and the authority of decision-making also leaves professional politicians too unaccountable for their actions, despite the formal requirement of a general election every four or more years. *The capacity to overcome the distance between people and decision-making power* is therefore our first criterion in arguing that crowdfunding represents a form of democratic finance.

The second form of democracy we introduce is based upon a *Participatory-Deliberative* model that aims to overcome that distance and has risen in popularity since the 1960s. This model is based upon a set of principles linked to concepts of political rights, most obviously the right to participate in the conduct of public affairs as enshrined in various international agreements.[29] The intention is that, by heeding to the wisdom of multiple voices from different communities of interest invited to participate in processes of decision-making, better governance structures can be created that will lead to fairer and more inclusive outcomes. This model is thus predicated on ideas of 'the public' and the 'common good', which are presumed to be widely shared, and so are guided by a belief that consensus is best achieved by acknowledging a plurality of perspectives. For this reason, participatory and deliberative ways of conducting public life have typically been adopted by national and supra-national organizations, such as the United Nations (UN) and European Commission (EC), when reaching decisions on a range of issues from poverty alleviation strategies to post-conflict peacebuilding. More recent examples include the phenomenon of citizens' juries, established to address a range of issues from the ethical use of artificial intelligence,[30] through to interrogating local cross-sector responses to the Climate Emergency.[31] Through these deliberative processes, opinions can and do change as a result of participation in collective discussion, receipt of greater information and the opportunity to learn what others think and value.

Since no model is perfect, however, the levels of active citizen involvement vary across processes. In some cases, people are empowered to exercise control over outcomes and thus hold a significant amount of power. In other cases, more consultative processes can often be tokenistic, providing little more than useful window-dressing whenever the veneer of citizen involvement is strategically useful to legitimate a decision already taken by those in charge. Though popular, this model of democracy risks minimizing or ignoring power differences during the process, including who feels (un)comfortable speaking in public, and so can fail to understand the importance of conflict over consensus in democratic life. Our second criterion to be considered, then, is the extent to which crowdfunding and P2P finance are transparently inclusive of more than just sophisticated investors, including *how far different people are enabled to hold significant power in determining outcomes from moving their money* into these alternative channels.

Finally, a *Radical-Agonistic* model of democracy steps in precisely to recognize the importance and inevitability of conflict in society, advocating for the need to embrace pluralism. In this model, civil society becomes a space for dissent, protest and resistance that exists beyond the control of market and state. It is here, in the heat of the *agora*, that opportunities emerge to challenge the legitimacy of any ruling order. From this perspective, choosing to engage in more formal processes of representative or deliberative democracy is in some sense seen as acquiescence to the status quo. Choosing to follow the formal rules of democratic participation is thus a form of subservience to a ruling elite, who have established more creative forms of government to manage such resistance in the face of burgeoning inequalities and injustices. At the more radical end of this model, the idea is to give up on the dream of ever achieving a rational consensus among the public and instead to accept the fundamental antagonisms that exist in the paradox between liberalism and democracy. Our third criterion for assessing crowdfunding and P2P finance, then, is how far they are able to *disrupt the power of entrenched elites and offer an alternative way for civil society to decide the various competing ways it may choose to provision what it needs*.

As well as establishing criteria for making our argument here, what we also learn from these three models of democracy is just how closely they also reflect the present crisis of mainstream finance. In continuing to hand over money to a professional class of financiers, as with casting a vote, people are left simply to hope that distant decisions will be taken in such a way that reflects their values. There isn't any meaningful opportunity in the current system truly to influence those professionals, who still remain largely unaccountable. In seeking alternatives through the innovations of crowdfunding and P2P finance, a choice needs to be made between greater levels of participation in finance and how far to radicalize civil society in order to check the power of neoliberal markets and states.

Wider ideals of financial democracy suggest that popular engagement should involve the empowerment of people in decision-making to claim the right to genuine control over economic issues. On the one hand, this may involve efforts to open up the private sector to public scrutiny, such as through corporate accountability and transparency processes and a growing culture of corporate social responsibility reporting.[32] On the other hand, there have been several attempts to engage people in local decision-making processes to generate new forms of public ownership to improve public services. Such efforts include municipal ownership schemes, co-operatives and community share offers, as well as employee ownership models. Throughout the remainder of this book, we want to argue that crowdfunding and P2P finance belongs in this list of alternative forms of democratic engagement. All three models of democracy provide a particular way to frame crowdfunding as a form of democratic finance, by enabling people to participate more actively in making decisions about how best to allocate money to projects that reflect their values.

What does finance value?

When faced with crisis, and so the requirement to decide upon a best way ahead, we are forced to confront the question: what do we really value? It is welcome, therefore, that such a question is not only being publicly raised by academics, but also by the 2020 BBC Reith Lecture Series that placed a very different kind of protagonist centre stage: Dr Mark Carney, former governor of the Banks of Canada (2008–13) and England (2013–20).[33] Carney opened this lecture series with a challenge to the conventions and values of the mainstream finance system of which, until recently, he had been one of the senior guardians. Finance, Carney argued, could no longer rely on the granting of its social licence as somehow automatic, enabling it to profit in perpetuity from the professional management and safeguarding of other people's money. The financial system is fast running the risk of no longer being fit for purpose if, Carney suggested, it failed to reform in order to respond to the 'triple threat' of Credit, COVID-19 and Climate.

Although understandable given by this time he was no longer in office, one of the most striking aspects of Carney's call for the rediscovery of finance's purpose as being to serve society in facing this 'triple threat' remains that it did not provoke the same howls of protest that greeted his previous economic briefings during the UK's referendum campaign to leave the European Union in 2016 ('Brexit'). Instead of professional outcry at the overtly 'political' nature of Carney's analysis, his words this time appeared to be met with solemn nods of approval. Could it be that many of those professionals working within the mainstream financial system feel as trapped and frustrated by its myths, structures and processes as those who are outside of it?[34]

Whatever the cause, the response to Carney's lectures was apparently one of widespread agreement that indeed finance could and should no longer treat the social and environmental costs of its investment decisions as somehow 'non-political', indeed 'non-financial', continuing to hold them at arm's length as mere 'externalities', to borrow the jargon of economists. How we invest is political. This is a key principle upon which we seek to position crowdfunding as a form of democratic finance. Better outcomes for people and planet ought to be the purpose of a finance system that is for society, since neither is an expendable resource to be burned up in its relentless and remorseless quest to accumulate only more of itself.

Carney's Reith lectures are significant, representing the first time that a senior leader of the global financial system has publicly raised the issue of finance's *purpose*, rather than obsessing over technical defences of its ability to *function*. The implications of Carney's insight, circulating as it does from the beating heart of the financial Leviathan, is that investment is and always has been a profoundly political act. Given this, it begs the question as to whose politics should decide upon the purpose of finance. In 2020, for example, the *Financial Times* reported that just 18 individuals sitting within professional finance and wealth management firms held sufficient power over bond markets to shift government policy on how and where to borrow and invest.[35] If we are to avoid a full-blown kleptocratic financial system, far more people are going to have to be included in meaningfully deciding upon the purpose of finance.

Returning to Carney's argument, what is significant is that as a former technocrat at the heart of the financial system he does not advocate for technocratic solutions to the 'triple threat' he identifies. As Carney carefully sets out in his first Reith lecture, we need to put aside Adam Smith's *The Wealth of Nations* – in Carney's own words, 'the most purchased, often cited and, arguably, least read books in the whole of economics' – and instead pick up Adam Smith's earlier book, *The Theory of Moral Sentiments*. This is because the social licence of finance rests not upon its technocratic power, but upon its democratic mandate. Carney recognizes this, and he goes a step further by suggesting that without this sense of purpose there is only questionable grounds for finance continuing to exist. Finance is not simply a money creating machine, since it also dictates the destination of money. If finance cannot respond to the triple threat to our democratic societies, then Carney asks bluntly: what is it for?

The values of mainstream finance continue to hold fast to the principles of neoliberalism, first turned into economic policy in the 1980s by Ronald Reagan in the USA and Margaret Thatcher in the UK.[36] Though variously interpreted, these values have become indisputable in the minds of most people, infecting all areas of our society and our politics. One of its principal ideas is that the safest way to eliminate political bias from policymaking is to enhance the unchecked power of apparently independent and democratically unaccountable finance professionals. Now outside of its most internal structures, Carney issues a challenge to those values of finance by seeking to reconnect morality with the idea of money.

Mainstream finance has seemingly lost its way, having become too inward-looking and obsessed by its own technical function to be sufficiently mindful of its public purpose. To the extent that it sees any purpose at all beyond investing in its own reproduction, those neoliberal values have led the system mistakenly into seeing its only purpose as being to grow further the wealth of the already wealthy. And, as the example of 'Super Mario' further demonstrates, the public too have come to fetishize the smooth functioning of the financial system to such an extent that they (also mistakenly) prefer to see it as a benevolent dictatorship, rather than a clear and present danger to the freedoms of our democratic societies.

In seeking a way forward, we suggest that the values and principles of alternative structures such as crowdfunding and P2P finance provide the best chance of rediscovering that purpose and renewing that social licence. We want to tell a different story about the social life of money, one which directly challenges the assumptions made within mainstream economics textbooks that prioritize the function of money and largely ignore its wider purpose. That story begins in the ancient city-state of Athens, but first our journey takes us on a tour of the global crowdfunding sector.

TWO

What is Crowdfunding?

In order to reveal how crowdfunding is different from mainstream finance, we first need to say something about the typical ways in which people understand and use their money. Since most people believe they cannot be trusted with money and so lack confidence when it comes to finance – a convenient story to tell people if you are running the financial system – it's important to begin our journey in familiar territory. After all, it is still the case that the average school leaver in the UK will have spent longer studying the mechanics of sexual reproduction than they will the workings of financial services products. Many young adults leave full-time education in the mistaken belief that a 'credit' card is somehow preferable to a 'debit' card – and who can blame them, when 'credit' is something that school teaches them to pursue, and 'debit' looks rather too much like the word 'debt' to be immediately reassuring. This confusion of a means of immediate payment with the idea of personal debt (actually acquired through using a credit card) does little to instil confidence.

This point is exaggerated along gender lines too. As we saw in Chapter One, women have been frequently positioned by mainstream finance as too emotional or irrational to be eligible for access to mainstream products like current and savings accounts. In a 2015 study by Abundance Investment, however, when investors were asked a question about the effects of inflation, or the risk of loss to housing equity from a drop in house prices, it was male respondents who were frequently mistaken in their calculations. Female respondents were far more likely to admit they didn't know the answer, and so only to select responses that they were relatively certain about. What this small study shows is that despite the assumptions of mainstream financial institutions, men are more likely to be 'confidently wrong' and women to be 'cautiously right', which perhaps hints that one of the main problems we face is who currently runs finance and who typically invests their money.

For the purposes of understanding where crowdfunding and P2P finance fits into our story, next we define some of the basic building blocks of the modern 'consumer' experience of money and finance. Rather than provide what would be a lengthy description of the different forms of financial product, which would test ours and the reader's patience, we will consider these familiar alternatives in terms of 'what money does'.

Savings accounts (in banks, building societies or National Savings)

Most money is usually held in either its cash form or on deposit with a bank in a savings account, which is typically guaranteed by the state via the central bank. In 2021, in the UK this guarantee is up to £85,000 and in the EU it is €100,000 euros per banking licence. This guarantees that money deposited can be readily convertible into cash 'on demand'. This is important because it forms the basis, perhaps the only basis, for how most people understand money and how it works. We assume that banks lend cash that we have deposited with them to other borrowers, but in reality there is no difference between the deposits we make as savers and the deposit account of a borrower when they take out a loan with a bank. This is because both are considered 'liabilities' – that is, money owed by the bank – on its balance sheet.

The idea that your savings with a bank or building society are being 'put to use', therefore, is not strictly true. Bank lending is dependent upon the capital which the bank holds, including equity, bonds and other forms of reserves (including cash) against the risk of loss should a borrower fail to repay their loan (or is at risk of default). In a building society, deposits from savers do form part of the capital that is held against the risk of loans going bad. National Savings also provide an alternative for savers to create deposits, this time directly guaranteed by the government, which accounts for these savings as liabilities and therefore part of the calculation of the national debt.

So, when it comes to regular savings on the high street, we can understand them as money held in reserve for immediate need. Whether in a bank, building society or National Savings account – and with apologies to the global film industry – this money is not backed by actual cash held in a vault somewhere in the institution. Instead, it is ultimately just a guarantee made by the state via the central bank.

Investments (capital at risk)

If savings are effectively passive money that carries little or zero risk, then money being at risk is called an investment. Investments come in three main forms. First, *equity*, which is a share in a company. This share confers a percentage ownership of a company that exists in perpetuity and so qualifies for a 'share' of the profits of the firm, which is called a 'dividend'. The second form is *debt*, usually as a bond or debenture. This is a formal IOU issued by a company, government or local authority that provides a certain payment of interest, called a 'yield', over a certain period of time, called 'maturity'. The third common form is a share not in a company, but in a *unit in a fund*. This is an entity that can hold financial and real assets (for example, a property) with the value of those assets affecting the value of those shares or units. This form of investment potentially pays an annual return, also known as a 'dividend'.

Investing in equity makes you a shareholder of the company and provides capital for that company to invest in creating or growing its business. Investing in debt (buying a bond or debenture) means that you are lending money to that company, project or government and is typically used to finance something specific, such as a new factory or a wind turbine. The exact terms of the bond or debenture give you certain rights over the capital and revenues of that entity to repay your investment and pay a return at a given point in the future. In both cases, your capital is at risk based on the success or failure of the company or project. A debt investment, however, will usually have priority over the money or assets of the company or project in the case of a problem arising, or the failure of the project versus the shareholders, and so is generally considered to be lower risk than an equity investment.

Savings accounts can be understood as essentially 'passive' because they don't confer any purpose on the money beyond those of the institution that is providing the guarantee that you can access the money as 'cash' when you need it. Investments, by contrast, are essentially 'active' since they give money purpose and as a result carry a risk that the value of your investment may be less in the future. Taking that risk is what qualifies you for potential financial returns, which can increase the value of your investment. For example, investment funds provide a means for investors to achieve a spread of risk and returns across a number of companies, projects and other assets. Your money is 'active' in the sense that the fund itself will have a strategy to invest, backing certain types of companies (that is, big or small start-ups) and projects (for example, green and social infrastructure, property construction and so on) on the basis that managing the 'pooled' or collective money of many investors gives a return that is not dependent on a single company, risk or outcome, but many 'diversified' investments. It is up to the investment or professional fund manager to decide what percentage of the total money pooled is exposed to what risk, impacting your potential financial return.

Given the low minimum thresholds available, crowdfunding as an investment creates new ways for more individuals to participate directly in supporting single companies, individuals or projects by making their own decisions on the level or percentage of money assigned to each – whether lending money to companies, individuals or projects, or buying a stake in a business or project. In all cases your money, or capital, is at risk and this justifies earning a return that is higher than holding your money in a savings account (which, given the state guarantee, are effectively risk free). At the other end of the scale, when you make a charitable donation to a good cause, then your money is considered to be fully at risk, in the sense that you don't actually seek any repayment.

The world of crowdfunding is incredibly diverse, however. There are two distinct types of crowdfunding platform, which we consider to be fundamental to the structure of the overall market and that set the context for our discussion in this chapter. The first is P2P finance, or more accurately P2P lending.[1] The second is crowdfunding itself. All platforms in these markets are based broadly on the original innovation created by the team that collectively inspired the first P2P platform, Zopa, in 2004.[2]

eBay for money

The original venture capital pitch for Zopa described it as 'eBay for money'. At the beginning of the 2000s, eBay was nearing its zenith and demonstrating how millions of individuals could thrive in online markets to meet their needs without high-street shopping. The insight that the team at Zopa were most keen to explore was the way in which eBay and similar auction websites promoted trust between strangers. They did this by creating a hybrid form of both market and community using the now ubiquitous star review rating system. While later incarnations of Zopa moved away from the ideal of a 'market of equals', which was the inspiration for the nomenclature 'peer to peer', the experiment was continued by new forms of crowdfunding platform that developed in Zopa's wake.

Just like buyers and sellers on eBay, platforms allow lenders and borrowers to connect with only a small and discrete risk exposure between them. Each loan is distributed to a group of lenders based upon the price at which they are willing to lend via different auction processes. In aggregate, these small decisions create an alternative system of credit for individuals and small- and medium-enterprises (SMEs) to that traditionally offered by banks. In the USA, this model is called 'marketplace lending', reflecting the different restrictions the regulator places upon the creation of new forms of market. This pushed P2P finance towards adopting a more formal model of securitization.[3] Zopa's own attempt to enter the US market tried to maintain some of the elements of the UK model by adopting the regulatory form of a credit union, but it was not able to compete successfully.

By contrast, crowdfunding was created to enable investors to back larger individual projects and businesses, with investments ranging from thousands to now millions of dollars in size. As with P2P markets, the principle of low minimum investment thresholds encourages any given fundraising campaign to seek thousands of investors, with each backing tens or hundreds of companies to deliver different blends of social, economic and environmental outcomes. Both crowdfunding and P2P platforms are thus built upon the idea that finance works best when people themselves decide what their money is used for. The story of Zopa is our first indication that the true value of money resides not in what money is, but in what money *does* and can be made to do differently.

While the pace of financial innovation has ebbed and flowed, occasionally leaving regulators in its wake, the principal ethos of platforms has stayed largely the same. Crowdfunding and P2P finance are built on distributed networks of people deciding to lend, borrow, invest and gift money in a manner that contrasts starkly with the formal structures that dominate the highly centralized practices of mainstream finance. Importantly, those individuals who engage with crowdfunding are deciding for themselves the purpose of their money. Refusing to place all of their trust into the hands of professional financiers, and retaining a greater say over the types of projects and businesses that get funded, crowdfunding investors are beginning to show the potential of democratizing finance. Before we get there, let's outline how crowdfunding actually works.

Crowdfunding: the basics

In its simplest expression, crowdfunding is 'a way of financing projects, businesses or loans through small contributions from a large number of sources, rather than large amounts from a few'.[4] Crowdfunding enables individuals to invest their money via online frameworks known as 'platforms'. These deposits commit a given amount of money in support of a specific project, business or loan. The minimum investment required to participate is usually very low – sometimes as low as £5 or US$10 – intended to make participation in crowdfunding accessible to the vast majority of potential investors or donors.

The relationship between those seeking funds and those willing to contribute funds is mediated by the company running the platform. It is worth making explicit that one of the principal attractions for fundraisers is that they can pursue a given financial target by acquiring lots of smaller amounts of money from many people ('the crowd'), rather than being beholden to the eligibility assessment criteria of a single bank or other mainstream lender. For those willing to allocate their money ('the funders'), the attraction is the ability to spread their risk by sharing out their money across multiple projects, as well as – and here is a key point for our wider argument – aligning their money more explicitly and transparently with their values by selecting which projects or businesses they wish to support. This is rarely an option when holding money in mainstream financial products and services, which simply operate in narrowly financial terms by offering only a given rate of return.

As the reader may be aware from their own experiences of crowdfunding, its most popular association is as a form of gift-making, allocating money via donation-based platforms to a wide range of charity appeals, creative arts projects or local independent business ventures. This has created a popular image of crowdfunding as being dominated by a 'hipster millennial crowd' of aspiring social entrepreneurs. This image has been hard to shake off,[5] but is now changing as more investment-based models begin to increase their share of the overall market by offering a rate of return on top of the ability to support social and environmental projects.

Today in the UK, a highly diverse ecosystem of crowdfunding platforms now operates, facilitating all manner of financial transaction: from P2P money lending to consumers (known as P2C) or to businesses (known as P2B, or 'marketplace' in the USA), through to selling shares ('equity crowdfunding') and gifting money to individuals or groups.[6] This gift can be in return for a 'thank you' of some sort, such as early access to an artist's new album or discounts on a new business's product line ('rewards-based crowdfunding'), or sometimes it is simply gifted to a good cause ('donation crowdfunding'). UK platforms first tend to develop a focus on a specific type of finance (for example donation, debt or equity), then subsequently diversify their focus to concentrate upon a specific sector of the economy, such as charity, real estate or infrastructure funding.

By investing in a company or project through a crowdfunding platform, however, it is possible to ensure that there is a much more transparent relationship between the funder and fundraiser, with both knowing precisely where and how their money is being used and to trust in that process. Put simply, when you put your money in a bank – through the kinds of high street savings and investment products already discussed – you are no longer the 'owner' of that money and the bank is able to direct its lending towards whomever it likes. It may lend it to arms dealers, choose to finance sweat shops or continue to invest in carbon-intensive industries. Clearly not all banks are doing this. But if the depositor knew how far removed the bank's lending decisions are from their motivations in handing over money, the public's perceptions of banks as 'safe' would risk being further undermined. The point to stress is that once money is deposited in a mainstream financial institution, there is really no way of knowing to what use the money has been put. A crowdfunding platform, on the contrary, allows the funder (as either lender or investor) to retain a far better idea of where the money is going, and crucially what it is being used for. In this sense, not only do individuals retain ownership and control of their money, but they can ensure that the purposes to which it is allocated are better aligned with their own values and the type of material projects they wish to make happen.

As already mentioned, we focus here upon the UK in outlining four major models of crowdfunding. In each case, we highlight the basic function and intended purpose of each model, and how they variously contribute to a democratization of finance.

Donation/rewards-based crowdfunding

These platforms facilitate the financing of individuals, charities or other smaller non-profit organizations. Investors see themselves as 'donors' and participate principally because they believe in a specific cause. They do not receive a financial return on their money, though they may receive other non-financial rewards. Donation-based platforms facilitate investment in everything from creative arts projects through to civic crowdfunding ventures tied to public infrastructure. Leading UK donation platforms are: Crowdfunder, who specialize in enabling individuals to back socially useful projects and activities; and SpaceHive, who enable investment in 'place-based' opportunities, such as improving derelict land or bringing a community asset back into use.[7]

Debt security or loans-based crowdfunding

These platforms facilitate the provision of debt finance to organizations and companies, bypassing the need for traditional banks. Depending on the specific business model of the platform, investors lend money via a loan or a debt security (bond/debenture). Investors see themselves as 'lenders', since they receive interest on the money they lend. If smooth, their capital is returned as either a single payment or as an annuity over the life of the investment. Platforms that deal in loans or debt securities are currently regulated under two related but separate regimes. Prior to 1 January 2020, debt securities sat within the EU-derived Markets in Financial Instruments Directive (MiFID) regime, whereas loans (known as 'P2P agreements') are governed by UK-specific legislation introduced in 2014 and updated in 2019, which is now somewhat cryptically called '36H'.[8] The debt category of crowdfunding is the most populated and diverse, which reflects the wide variety of use cases for debt financing within the economy.

Leading UK platforms include Abundance Investment, a debt security platform focused on providing short and long-term debt to infrastructure companies and public sector organizations. Abundance was co-founded by Bruce Davis, one of the authors of this book. Funding Circle are another successful loan-based platform focused on providing working capital and growth capital to the UK's SME sector. Funding Circle were the first P2P lender to float on the London Stock Exchange in 2019. The original P2P lender, offering loans to consumers rather than to businesses, was Zopa that was founded in 2004 and launched in March 2005. Since then, Zopa has significantly innovated and diversified its business, including the acquisition of a full banking licence, provisionally acquired with restrictions in 2018 and granted on 24 June 2020.[9]

Equity-based crowdfunding

These platforms support equity-based capital raising by new or established businesses who offer shares, rather than bonds or loans. Currently, the sector is focused primarily upon the 'early-stage' or 'start-up' phase of company growth, so investors typically hope their shares will increase in value. Crowdcube is a leading UK equity crowdfunding platform for entrepreneurs of start-ups and growing businesses to connect with potential investors. Seedrs was the UK's first regulated equity-based crowdfunding platform, enabling investors to buy shares in early-stage high-growth businesses.[10] Between them, the platforms have raised more than £2 billion for businesses including money from conventional venture capital firms investing alongside individuals.

Co-operatives and community benefit societies

A smaller UK market exists for both co-operative (Co-ops, also known as Industrial and Provident Societies) and community benefit society ('Bencom') business models. Although there are subtle differences between the two, in practice they are extremely similar. Technically, a co-operative is run for the benefit of its members, whereas a benefit society is run for the benefit of the community. Both use withdrawable shares, known as 'community shares', which are often managed via a crowdfunding platform. This model is nevertheless distinct from traditional equity investing as the share offers are currently exempt from regulation by the Financial Conduct Authority (FCA). The model is underpinned by the idea of equality in terms of governance, with one shareholder getting one vote regardless of investment level, rather than a vote-per-share process typical with traditional equity models. Ethex are one of the UK's leading platforms in this sector, having pioneered the concept of 'positive investing'.[11] While these models do exist in the crowdfunding space, as Ethex have proven very successfully, the majority of activity within the co-operative space concerns the issuance of community shares, rather than strict equity-based crowdfunding.

The variety of crowdfunding platforms that exist represents the variety of motivations among individuals who are prepared to donate, lend or invest, and what outcomes they wish their money to deliver. These motivations and expectations, both in terms of the function and purpose of that money, is captured by the different models of crowdfunding that operate in the market. As these four major models demonstrate, the perception of crowdfunding as just another form of gift-making or philanthropy is too narrow and already somewhat dated. Among the many different forms of crowdfunding that exist are those that provide an alternative and regulated form of financial investment.[12] For these models, the appeal of crowdfunding is how it helps to bypass traditional bank lending criteria. Investment-based crowdfunding enables more immediate funding to be received from a crowd of highly dispersed 'lenders/investors', and to be transparently allocated to highly differentiated categories of 'borrowers/projects', all via an online platform or smartphone app. This practice stands in sharp contrast to the more mainstream activity of individuals and businesses having to approach high-street banks and other institutional lenders in order to raise funding. Of course, both platforms and investors carry out their own due diligence on who to lend to and borrow from, and – just as with eBay – there is always a risk that the person on the other end cannot be trusted. But such incidences are rare and, to the confusion of many mainstream economists, social systems of trust continue to function perfectly well without a formal intermediary.

In being explicitly linked to specific projects or loans, crowdfunding provides a viable alternative to handing over money to banks and financial institutions in the hope (rather than the expectation) that they will invest that money responsibly and in ways that align with the depositor's values. Indeed, an internet search quickly reveals a bewildering array of causes seeking to raise money through different crowdfunding models – from seeking help with health care or college tuition fees, through to holidays, veterinary bills, help with settling legal fees, or releasing amateur films and music. More typically, crowdfunding offers new financial channels for moving money in support of a wide range of activities – including general business finance, property development, renewable energy and community projects – facilitating the transfer of hundreds of thousands (and sometimes millions) in investment for single projects.[13]

Those investors who allocate funds are often doing so because of the promise that their money will be invested in projects more transparently aligned with a stated social or environmental mission. This reflects a growing motivation among so-called 'responsible investors' to pursue a more blended return of both financial and non-financial outcomes through their engagement with crowdfunding platforms.[14] In contrast, P2P loans are a simple act of lending but with the platform connecting the fundraiser with the funder without the need for a bank to intermediate. Money is thus not lent or borrowed on the basis of credit or leverage, but merely transferred back and forth. In this respect, crowdfunding and P2P may be interpreted as signalling the possibility for a return to 'pre-capitalist' (or at least pre-modern) lending practices, which existed for centuries without the need for any formal banking system. Indeed, as we will see in Chapter Three, similar arrangements to P2P lending can be found in ancient Athens and were adopted by the government of Victorian Britain to boost investment in public infrastructure long before the advent of high-street banking for the public.

Given these historical precedents for moving money in ways that did not require complex banking practices, we suggest that crowdfunding is founded upon a long-standing set of democratic principles that can point the way towards a radically different future for finance beyond simply trying to reform the mainstream system. As Jonathan Bone et al have shown, it is the simplicity, transparency and lack of leverage inherent in models of crowdfunding and P2P lending that has already attracted those campaigning for financial reform.[15] What is undoubtedly new, however, are the ways in which technological innovations are further digitizing the mainstream and alternative financial systems while also transforming access to finance by lowering barriers to entry for people. This opens up the possibility for different and disruptive ways of funding and fundraising without the need for formal financial institutions, with the result that individuals, communities and businesses are engaging more seriously with crowdfunding markets all around the world.

As we are arguing throughout this book, one explanation for the growth in crowdfunding activity is a widespread loss of trust in the current institutions of both democracy and finance, which still remain largely unchanged more than a decade on from the 'starting gun' events of 2008,[16] and which has been further intensified by responses to the global COVID-19 pandemic. The lack of accountability and democratic control over mainstream finance, which we saw in Chapter One led Silvia Walby to argue is what caused the events of 2008, is one of the reasons why crowdfunding platforms have been able to position themselves as 'alternative, disruptive, or democratizing'.[17] For us, we see genuine potential in crowdfunding to be all three – and in particular, democratizing – when seen in the long wave of financial innovations throughout human history, which have likewise tended to emerge in response to states of emergency. Having looked in detail at the different models of crowdfunding operating the UK, let's now look in more detail at the size and volume of crowdfunding activity around the world.

Crowdfunding around the world and back

While the UK crowdfunding sector is our primary case study, it is also the case that there are now burgeoning crowdfunding markets in the Americas, Africa and the Middle East, China and the Asia-Pacific, and Europe.[18] To give an immediate sense of scale, the total value of the overall crowdfunding market in the UK grew 30 per cent year on year to US$10.4 billion during 2018, up from US$8 billion in 2017 and from US$6 billion in 2016. These figures, and those that follow, are quoted from research conducted by the Cambridge Centre for Alternative Finance (CCAF) and are based upon the question-naire responses of more than 1,200 companies and more than 2,700 platforms across more than 180 countries.[19]

According to CCAF, the global crowdfunding and P2P finance (both marketplace and lending) sectors were worth US$304.5 billion in 2018. More than US$215 billion of that volume is accounted for by the substantial, but seemingly highly volatile, alternative finance market in China. The Chinese market has grown rapidly during the last decade without recourse to formal regulations in a way that would be recognized in Western economies. More recently, however, the Chinese market has been increasingly subject to state interven-tion that has correlated with a significant (and relatively sudden) downturn in reported volumes of business. CCAF measure that decline as being more than US$100 billion from 2017. CCAF also estimate the global volume of alternative finance outside of China as continuing to see strong growth, however, with the global market data showing a rise of 48 per cent from 2017 (US$60 billion) to 2018 (US$89 billion). Excluding China, according to CCAF the biggest markets globally are the US (US$61 billion in 2018) and the UK (US$10.4 billion in 2018). Five other countries now register more than US$1 billion of alternative finance volumes, including Australia, Germany, Indonesia, Japan and the Netherlands.

In Europe, although the UK is still the largest market by some margin, the total online crowdfunding market has grown steadily with overall volumes rising from US$1.5 billion in 2013 to US$18.1 billion in 2018. The Asia-Pacific region has also seen strong growth. Excluding China from this data, volumes have increased 69 per cent from US$3.64 billion to US$5.90 billion between 2017 and 2018. Africa and the Middle East have followed a similar pattern. The Middle Eastern alternative finance market has increased year-on-year, up 131 per cent from US$346.5 million in 2017 to $800.5 million in 2018. The African market grew by 102 per cent, rising from US$103.8 million in 2017 to US$209.1 million in 2018. Interestingly, unlike other global regions, Africa currently has no single dominant market in a specific country.

While this quantitative data is clearly useful for establishing the size and volume of crowdfunding around the world, what is more significant still is how the global reach of crowdfunding as an idea is helping to diversify the financial system through helping to build a narrative that a more 'moral economy' is possible. As more and more people choose to move their money out of traditional channels and into crowdfunding and P2P finance, the potential to disrupt habitual financial behaviours and change the purpose of money only grows. Since platforms typically promote their activities as a 'moral alternative' to mainstream finance, a broader social movement has emerged that seeks to construct disruptive forms of finance that are capable of driving investment for more positive social and environmental change in a way that places far greater emphasis on citizen participation and ownership within local communities.

Returning to the UK, an example of this broader movement is the emergence of a vibrant community of civil society groups campaigning for a more moral form of finance. This includes both trade associations – for example, the UK Crowdfunding Association (UKCFA), the Innovate Finance 36H Group and the UK Business Angels Association (UKBAA)[20] – and a dynamic and imaginative network of researchers, policy analysts and activists, with the most prominent being Compass, Economic Change Unit, Finance Innovation Lab, Institute for Public Policy Research (IPPR), Make My Money Matter, New Economics Foundation (NEF), New Economy Organisers Network (NEON), Positive Money, Share Action and Tax Justice.[21] We regard the relationships between UK crowdfunding platforms and this wider campaign movement as highly significant because it signals a proactive attempt to police the dividing line between alternative finance and the mainstream. If the sector is to represent a more democratic alternative to mainstream channels, then this civil society network will continue to be crucial in providing an important moral compass to keep crowdfunding platforms on track.

The relationship between forms of crowdfunding and P2P finance to regulation has been more complex. The UK is generally recognized as having one of the most sophisticated regulatory approaches to crowdfunding and P2P finance, which has been widely copied around the world. But even here, there are tensions between the challenges for regulators who are faced with an innovative system of finance that is more accessible to ordinary retail investors, and how they themselves are enabled to enforce the rules to protect a vastly increased body of customers from poor practice or even deliberate financial harm.

As mentioned previously, the UK's crowdfunding and P2P finance sectors are regulated by the FCA, which over the past few years has adopted varying levels and types of approach to innovations in crowdfunding. There is also wider oversight from a range of public sector bodies and government departments, such as HM Treasury and ultimately the Bank of England.[22] The experience of crowdfunding and P2P finance working with finance regulation provides a useful insight into the barriers that exist to meaningful innovation and the development of public value. These are highlighted in the following Mission Statement from spring 2017, when the FCA appeared to signal a commitment to supporting a more socially oriented financial system. Specifically, the statement included a chapter on 'Public Value' that outlines an urgent need to rebuild trust in financial markets, stating:

> Public value is the collective value that an organisation contributes to society. This is in contrast to private or market value, which is the value of a good or service to an individual customer and provider. Our aim is to add public value by improving how financial markets

operate, to benefit individuals, businesses and the UK economy.[23]

Before examining this relationship further, it is important to establish the difference between what we have described as P2P lending (which the FCA calls 'loans based crowdfunding') and investment-based crowdfunding where the platform facilitates (or 'arranges' in the jargon of investments) shares, debentures and bonds that have been subject to financial regulation since the practice was first formalized in the UK in the 19th century. P2P lending, when it launched in 2005, was not regulated by the UK's then Financial Services Authority (the predecessor to the FCA). Indeed, the UK crowdfunding sector has long lobbied for greater understanding and regulation of its practices. As the sector grew in size, platforms wanted to ensure that the standards of new entrants were being overseen by the UK's financial watchdog, but the appetite from both the regulator and government at that time was reportedly dismissive.

Investment-based crowdfunding was regulated from the outset, however, since the products involved were captured by existing definitions of investment products (unlike P2P loans). In 2011, the first platforms to be regulated were Abundance Investment (debenture – a type of bond – based investments), Seedrs (shares) and Crowdcube (shares). It was not until 2014 that a single unifying framework was created by the FCA, which provided a basis for the different forms of crowdfunding and P2P finance to come under the aegis of the regulator. At that point, the FCA was mindful of its newly acquired parliamentary objective to ensure competition in financial markets, to provide new forms of business finance at the same time as improving choice for those investors seeking a complementary alternative to the public stock markets. A number of high-profile initial public offerings (IPOs) – which are the first time a company's shares can be bought by anyone – had demonstrated just how much financial institutions had the technology and capital to extract significant advantages over

vestors, a situation that triggered the GameStop
021.[24]

etween 2016 and 2019, however, the FCA conducted perhaps the most detailed and far-reaching review of the crowdfunding and P2P finance sector, with one of the authors, Mark Davis, the lead researcher of a team based at Leeds and Cambridge universities mandated by the FCA to get under the skin of the sector to understand how the new rules were working for investors in practice. In 2019, that review concluded that P2P lending should be moved to a similar level of regulation as investment-based crowdfunding, which now requires platforms to conduct a test for all investors to assess their understanding (called 'appropriateness'), to categorize all investors according to the innovative framework developed in 2014,[25] and placed restrictions on how platforms marketed investments. It also concluded that the regulator was 'broadly content' with the effectiveness of the rules for investment-based crowdfunding.

As we move into the middle of 2021, the political fallout from a number of high-profile failures of 'unregulated' investments – including the case of London Capital and Financial (LCF), which offered so-called 'minibonds' to investors promising high returns with only minimal protections (allegedly also making false claims about the eligibility of such investments for the UK's Innovative Finance ISA scheme) – has shifted the focus of the regulator away from innovation and competition and towards customer protection. A review of the LCF case, which was carried out by Dame Gloster QC as an independent judge, presumably provided uncomfortable reading for the regulator and those individuals in its senior management who were named in the report.[26] Dame Gloster detailed several occasions when either the regulator failed to heed warnings about the investments or did not understand the nature of the investments being offered.

The impact of the LCF scandal has been damaging to the reputation of the UK sector, in terms of both media and customer perception, but also in terms of new rules that have effectively banned certain types of investment from being offered (mainly relating to property construction). What is less clear at the time of writing is how much this will detract from the FCA's 2017 strategy to focus the regulator on creating public value, and how much the development of crowdfunding will be viewed through the perspective of failures by the regulator to enforce existing rules that were designed to ensure individuals have the freedom and opportunity to invest their money in line with their values. With that cautionary note firmly struck, in the final section we return to the idea of democratizing finance.

Crowdfunding as 'democratic finance'

In Chapter One, we introduced three models of democracy that each pointed to an important criterion for assessing the potential of crowdfunding to democratize finance. We are not the first to explore this connection, however, with the *Economist* magazine being the first establishment voice to do so.[27]

In 2014, the American sociologist Fred L. Block also set out an agenda for what 'democratic finance' could and should look like, stating that 'there is an urgent need for ideas about how finance could be reorganized to disempower the existing financial elite'.[28] Block highlights how the global financial system is deliberately constructed to ensure the vast majority of private savings and investments pass through mainstream financial institutions, as outlined earlier in this chapter. As a result, the destination of money is shaped by a very narrow range of channels controlled by a financial elite through banks, pension funds and so on. This allows for significant transaction fees to be extracted, totalling more than US$650 billion per annum as we also saw in Chapter One.

Block argues that any attempt to 'democratize finance' would first need 'to shrink the major financial institutions' by creating 'new financial channels so that private savings could be directed to overcome the shortage of financing' in areas of 'systematic underinvestment' by mainstream lenders. The areas Block identifies are those vital to meeting the grand challenges of the 21st century, namely: clean and renewable energy, deep retrofit of residential and commercial building stock, green small- and medium-enterprises, and other large public infrastructure projects across health, transport and the renewal of public space. This democratizing reform of the financial system, he argues, would also create the regulatory space for building alternative economic infrastructures by fighting for more political representation, as well as – and significantly for our argument here – finding new ways to encourage the public to move their money into new financial channels. According to Block, this would:

> open the path for the construction of a different kind of economy that would enhance the power of local communities, put greater emphasis on equality and social inclusion, and prioritize significant movement towards environmental sustainability. In short, democratizing finance … could simultaneously weaken the power of entrenched elites while moving society toward an economy that is subordinated to democratic political initiatives.[29]

It is immediately apparent how Block's framing of democratic finance aligns very well with the principles and practices of crowdfunding and P2P finance. In setting out his vision, Block's rallying cry stands commendably at odds with those who have little more to offer than a defeated shrug when faced with the awesome power of mainstream finance. Like Block, we believe that the case for radical reform of the global financial system is obvious, but instead we argue that the potential of crowdfunding remains under-explored as one of the more realistic and practical tools for delivering that reform.

After all, the freedom to move money remains one of the more curiously overlooked aspects of the events of 2008. At the time, high street banks and financial institutions – so obviously at the heart of those risky practices that appeared to bring the world suddenly to its economic knees – caused widespread public outrage by refusing to suspend their payment of bonuses, or to downgrade payments made as shareholder dividends. Their daringly swift return to 'business as usual' was curiously mirrored by the public's equally nonchalant return to normal life as if nothing had happened. In spite of the public outrage at mainstream finance, cited in almost every poll of the time as the 'least trusted' institution in society, people nevertheless continued to hand over their money to those same institutions. If banks simply carried on as before, well, just as alarmingly, so did we.

It is important to remember that there remain many noble elements of the banking profession, from the long hours of those working in branches and call centres, through to those who diligently assess someone's capacity to borrow for a new home or a business loan. But far removed from the bricks and mortar reality of high-street bank branches, the culture of finance within those gleaming towers of the City of London and Wall Street meant that banking as an institution was now beholden to its elite shareholders and so the vicissitudes of financial capital, rather than to its day-to-day depositors and creditors. It was this culture, devoid of any meaningful accountability to the public and driven in large part by the 'big swinging dicks' of a financialized masculinity,[30] that led to the collapse of trust in mainstream finance and the call for its urgent democratization.

It in this context that we focus upon crowdfunding as one of those new channels laying claim to being able already to provide a viable and more democratic alternative to mainstream finance. In assessing its democratizing potential, against those three criteria set out in Chapter One, we see crowdfunding as both one of the world's newest financial innovations and as based upon some of its oldest democratic ideas and principles. Indeed, the introduction of P2P finance itself was accompanied with an image not of the internet but of the view of the Acropolis and the site of the Athenian Assembly on the slopes of the Pnyx from the Agora of Athens in the 5th century BCE.

In making our case, we want to be clear that we do not consider crowdfunding to be a 'silver bullet', capable of magically solving all of the world's problems in an instant. The future of our democracies does not hinge on the success or failure of crowdfunding markets. What we do claim, however, and in the spirit of work led by J.K. Gibson-Graham, is that there are already alternative financial practices underway in the here and now that point to a different set of values and that are capable of gathering momentum and scaling further.[31] Crowdfunding is very much part of a wider ecosystem that could radically shift the balance of economic and political forces in favour of people and planet. It is not inevitable that finance has to be organized in the way it presently is, primarily serving the needs of an elite with little incentive to align itself with the needs of the many.

And, we are not alone in seeing genuine potential here. Others have already pointed to crowdfunding's capacity to increase local economic resilience, to finance community development projects, and to strengthen the resolve of the overall financial system by encouraging far greater levels of public engagement and participation.[32] By enhancing the participation of the many in making financial decisions that impact their community, and so taking a greater share of overall control over the flow of resources within a local economy, crowdfunding would seem to meet one of the key components for a democratic finance as put forward by Block.

To date, however, there has been no systematic study of crowdfunding that explores its history and theorizes its present by utilizing sociological and anthropological accounts of money. Before we come to those tasks in subsequent chapters, we first conclude our tour by looking at who is already participating in the UK's crowdfunding sector and, just as importantly, who isn't.

Democratizing finance? For whom, about what?

As we have shown, the democratization of finance includes the extension of greater oversight and control of the financial system by other democratic institutions, such as national and local governments, but chiefly by citizens themselves.[33] Translated into the practice of crowdfunding platforms, democratization is taken to involve widening participation in the financial system, opening up areas of financial activity that were previously the preserve of a small, wealthy and informed elite of investors. In this way, the idea of democratic finance is often translated as 'financial inclusion'. On the one hand, accessibility to a greater range of financial options can appear to be a positive step for those who are presently marginalized. By lowering the barriers to participation, opportunities are created for the wider public to lend or invest in businesses when they may previously have lacked the funds, knowledge or contacts to do so.

But this can also be too hasty a conclusion to draw, since inclusion in a financial system that is set up to exploit and extract value from those who come within its purview is clearly problematic. As Rajiv Prabhakar has recently argued, the inclusion of marginalized and disadvantaged groups in the world of finance and asset ownership is neither good nor bad, but potentially dangerous.[34] While greater financial inclusion is clearly a way of helping people to navigate everyday decisions about money, at the same time there is a genuine risk of further areas of public life becoming subject to processes of financialization with more citizens becoming consumers of financial goods and services. Indeed, the very emergence of crowdfunding as an alternative to mainstream finance is a clear signal that to be included within a system proven to be exploitative of both people and planet is either a risk or an opportunity to change it from the inside.

It is certainly problematic to equate crowdfunding with those democratic models of *participation* and *deliberation* introduced in Chapter One and weakly conclude that this is automatically 'a good thing'. Furthermore, the ambition for full financial inclusion through greater participation in online crowdfunding platforms already presupposes access to the internet and the right to a bank account. Even in our hyper-connected age, there remains a stark digital divide throughout societies whereby large numbers of people remain 'unbanked' and exist without reliable broadband, a situation that the COVID-19 pandemic has thrown into sharper relief. For these reasons, crowdfunding platforms do not typically claim to be addressing the problem of 'financial exclusion' and there are precious few claims that crowdfunding could or should address the structural causes of this problem. Creating alternative opportunities for more sections of society to have a meaningful say in redirecting existing savings and investments into more productive social and environmental projects in their community is, however, an important component in democratizing finance.

In this way, crowdfunding can play a role in stimulating public engagement in projects that genuinely meet the needs of citizens in a given community and thus are more likely to be a partner in funding community, third sector and local authority projects.[35] The democratization of finance could ultimately be aimed at involving and empowering the public to make decisions within crowdfunding platforms themselves, adopting a more co-operative or mutual ownership type of business model. The practice of engaging your prospective investor market in the design, funding and implementation of a project as a measure of popular support for a given venture is already seen to increase the chances of a successful crowdfunding offer.[36] Yet the majority of UK crowdfunding platforms have not yet introduced more inclusive governance models, based upon an equality of voting power, and instead continue to operate on a 'one pound one vote' basis, rather than a 'one member one vote' system that would help to manage imbalances in power and influence within an organization.

Indeed, those older alternative finance models of co-operatives, mutuals and credit unions, advocated by Block as a way of best prioritizing the needs of local people, would seem to get far closer to the ideals of democratizing finance when equated with fairer ownership and more inclusive governance structures. One of crowdfunding's contributions to this wider ecosystem of alternatives to mainstream finance is to open up new possibilities for channelling money into positive investments that can also reach people who are less inclined to become actively involved in the governance of such structures.

Furthermore, any process of democratizing finance has to confront the temptation to fixate on a perceived lack of financial literacy among the general public. It is frequently the case that the problems of the financial system are individualized in this way, with blame squarely heaped upon the shoulders of people who we are told simply do not understand the complexities of money and finance sufficiently to be trusted with a greater level of control and ownership over decision-making processes. Although not against the idea of a public education programme in money and finance – one of our hopes for this book is that people will never again look at their money in quite the same way – we argue strongly against attributing blame to individuals. Rather than the public needing to learn more about finance, we propose the contrary view – namely, that mainstream finance needs to overcome its relative ignorance of the social relations, underlying motives and budgeting competencies of the public and to cease reducing them to abstracted behavioural models that presuppose rational calculations of optimizing financial outcomes. To do so would be a giant leap towards rediscovering its purpose in the service of people and planet.

Establishing such a commitment to direct productive investment is a principal motivation among a growing community of crowdfunding investors.[37] To be truly democratic and accessible, more needs to be done to encourage non-typical investors to engage with the sector. Those who do participate remain largely male, White, over 55 years of age and retired. Mindful of the risks of financial inclusion already stated, without greater and more diverse participation investment patterns will continue only to reflect the worldviews of this extremely narrow section of the population, which is highly unlikely also to reflect the views of women, different ethnic groups, the young and those trying to balance work with caring responsibilities. What might the world look like if the values of these groups were more actively driving investment decisions?

While the online nature of crowdfunding platforms may suggest a form of democratization based upon greater spatial openness and inclusivity as financial barriers to entry continue to be lowered, so far this has not resulted in overcoming a marked regional bias as the UK sector is overwhelmingly concentrated in London and the South-East of England. One of the opportunities presented by the sector's heavy reliance on the internet is to help overcome the limitations of local fundraising, while at the same time avoiding every local group or business having to apply to a London-based organization. Nevertheless, the regional biases in the circulation of funds and the concentration of company headquarters in London, suggests that the UK sector's practice still has some way to go in this regard. Other global regions face similar concentrations of activity and it is currently an open question as to whether crowdfunding can find a resolution to this challenge in a way that overcomes, rather than helps to exaggerate and further entrench, existing regional inequalities. For example, there is an acknowledgement that wealthier areas are able to invest more funds and so drive more projects to better their local communities, whereas those areas that lack resources to invest fall further behind.

Importantly, in striving to democratize finance through empowering local communities to drive forward productive investment in their area, the relationship between crowdfunding platforms and the public appears to be increasingly symbiotic. This is both in terms of providing the money to be moved into identified projects, and also in terms of goodwill, support, and devoting time and skills to delivering intended outcomes of public value.

Recognizing that currently the public have very little, if any, direct say in what happens to their money once it is handed over to a mainstream financial institution, crowdfunding platforms in the UK have made direct appeals to customers by promising to provide an alternative to dealing with the opaque 'black box' of high-street banks. Crowdfunding promises a simple way for people to take control of their own money and to think carefully about where it is invested and how it could be used to build something real and tangible to make a better world for citizens, rather than lining the pockets of entrenched elites. The traditional process is fundamentally disempowering and undemocratic, as the investor defers all responsibility to a financial institution and grants them the power to decide how their money is utilized, with no direct influence over the many potential outcomes that are created by that investment.

In order to establish further the credibility of claiming that these processes qualify crowdfunding as a form of democratic finance, in Chapter Three we trace a history of the relationship between the public and its money to begin to expose some of the myths and stories about both that have shaped the relationship between finance and politics for centuries.

THREE

Democratic Finance, Then and Now

The rise of crowdfunding and P2P finance in the 21st century has been driven in part by its public promise to facilitate the democratization of finance. At the same time, and in a radically different direction, we have seen a massive concentration of the power over wealth in the mainstream finance industry. As described in Chapter One, we see this concentration as resembling Hobbes's figure of Leviathan in the scale of its influence and reach over our lives.

The growth of this new financial Leviathan, and the redrawing of the social contract by which we negotiate our individual and collective well-being, has occurred at the same time as a widespread collapse in trust – in the state, in democracy and in finance itself. This collapse has placed responsibilities for managing the various trials of daily life increasingly onto already burdened individual shoulders, both in terms of the here and now and in making sufficient provision for later life. In turn, as trust has been lost in the capability of our institutions to protect and provide for us, individuals have chosen to place their trust – that is, their money – into the financial Leviathan, without whose benevolent protection they would be forced to face the future war of all against all from the position of a life that is 'nasty, precarious, and skint' (to misquote Hobbes).

In these times of rapid change and uncertainty, we have thus become beholden to a decreasing number of companies who we are empowering to make decisions that affect much of the world's wealth and how it is used. In handing over our trust in the form of our money, professional financiers can command significant fees based on the power they wield. Those fees not only reflect the market power that the finance industry commands, but also its political power. Timely, then, that we should consider whether such a situation is healthy for our democracies and the long-standing principles and values that underpin them.

The question of who controls money, and so the best system for ensuring that its benefits outweigh its costs and risks, is one which has been asked by philosophers, historians and the writers of theatrical comedies since ancient times. Telling the story of that history is the main purpose of this chapter. Before we venture back there, however, we begin by asking why it is that we seemingly find it so difficult to trust ourselves when it comes to managing our own money.

Who controls your money?

Money is a system of mutual trust. It is how we are able to negotiate with those we know and with strangers we don't over the goods and services that we require. Only because we can trust that the other person also recognizes a given object as being 'money' – whether it be a shell, a stick, a nugget of mineral or a piece of paper – can we be assured that they will enter an exchange by accepting our means of payment. If we tried to pay for a bag of barley with a pint of milk, we'd be relying upon the owner of the barley either to want the milk for themselves, or to know someone who needed milk and who also owned something the barley owner needed. As is evident, this system quickly gets complicated and closes off options for exchange. But since everyone knows that everyone wants money, everyone can trust in the object called 'money'.

Given the entire system of money is little more than a physical or virtual representation of trust, it is curious that so often we don't actually trust ourselves when it comes to managing money. As a result, it is the ability to decide what money actually does, and who is best placed to manage it in the public interest, that is handed over to professional financiers when we participate in the mainstream system. Simply put, we abdicate responsibility for all but the most basic decisions over money. Even though the financial system has placed such enormous strains on our environment, our democratic systems of government, and our daily lives toiling in more or less precarious employment between countless other caring responsibilities, the appeals to address the social licence of finance and its power over our money continue to resound only with a deafening silence.

When reform of the finance industry is discussed, there is a tendency to focus somewhat narrowly upon the efficiency and *function* of the system, rather than on questioning the *purpose* and legitimacy of its activities. Although a great deal of importance is often placed upon the nature of competition within the market for financial products, the same cannot be said when it comes to the political implications of an elite few making an increasing number of the key decisions about the future well-being of society and the planet. As this power becomes increasingly concentrated into a smaller number of institutions, and with a smaller number of individuals wielding extreme influence, there are urgent questions to be asked about the legitimacy of such a massive concentration of power in a free and democratic society. While we have seen already that different models of democracy exist, each one is built upon the idea of 'the many' being represented, participating or being able to form relations in civil society to hold power radically to account. On that basis, such a concentration of wealth, power and influence in the hands of so few can only be seen as non-democratic, if not also anti-democratic.

This accumulation of wealth and how it is, or more frequently isn't, invested in the interests of people and planet takes on a still greater significance when we recognize that four decades of privatization and financialization have seen a massive shift in the requirement for citizens to assume greater responsibility to provide for their own financial resilience. The embeddedness of neoliberal policymaking has replaced social and public service provision with market-oriented and profit-driven alternatives.[1] This has seen more areas of public goods and services, once funded through collective taxation and accessed by virtue of citizenship, become privatized and so now only accessible through various forms of consumer credit. Reflecting on those four decades, Mary Mellor explains that: 'Citizens became consumers. Employee rights became zero-hours contracts. Welfare support became scrounging. Houses became investment opportunities. Debt became a way of life. The state became a dependent "household".'[2] In 2020, the value of the UK's retirement wealth, for example, surpassed that of the value of our residential property wealth for the first time.[3] We have never been so empowered and at the same time so powerless over our money.

This fundamental relationship between finance and democracy is complicated still further when we notice a truth hidden in plain sight – the financial system today is frequently reliant upon emergency levels of state support. This is as true of those colossal bailouts[4] of 'too big to fail' banks delivered through monetary policy measures in 2008, and subsequently labelled as 'quantitative easing' (QE),[5] as it is of the requirement for the state to underwrite guarantees on the system of retail bank savings, as we saw in Chapter Two. In other words, when banks are cited as being worthy of our trust because they remain the safest place to hold money, what this actually means is that the system of state-backed guarantees to protect deposits is worthy of our trust. This point is worth stressing, since the idea that it is a bank that 'keeps' or 'holds' money safely in a big vault to protect it from nefariously minded others remains one of the most pernicious myths that helps the financial system to reproduce itself. The myth endures for no less significant a reason than to maintain (or to buy) the public's trust in the entire financial system.

Such emergency measures were implemented in the desperate days following the collapse of Lehman Brothers and

Northern Rock in 2008 when, according to the account of former UK Chancellor of the Exchequer, Alistair Darling, 'we were 24 hours away from the ATMs running out of cash'.[6] The 'money' to pay for these interventions came from governments and central banks via all the technical means under their control, but crucially it was a *political* decision and not an economic one to put taxpayers and the users of public services on the hook for the 'bill'. As is well-documented, this has resulted in more than a decade of austerity policies that have further undermined trust in democracy, while cutting public spending is once again being mooted as vital to save our economies from the devastating impact of the COVID-19 pandemic.

Part of the problem here, we suggest, is that the cultural memory of what happens in financial crises is often short and incomplete because their root causes and true costs are made to seem so complex and opaque. Readers living in the UK may remember spending night after night in 2008 listening carefully to the BBC's Economics Editor Robert Peston speaking in solemn tones on the evening's *10 o'clock News*, but the actual substance of his idiosyncratic descriptions were so unfamiliar that they quickly receded from public memory. Instead, the newly minted jargon and acronyms were quickly normalized as pregnant descriptions of functionally and politically complex financial operations and, as anger gave way to ennui, we simply returned to trusting experts who surely must understand those words to manage our money.

Zygmunt Bauman formed the view that these actions on the part of world leaders amounted to nothing less than the truly remarkable creation of a 'welfare state for the rich'.[7] Assembled in an instant by immediately employing the full might and willingness of global states to act in order to protect the vested interests of an elite few, as a consequence the legitimate daily demands of the many were once again simply brushed aside and left for another day. Furthermore, while the regular welfare state for the poor continued to be underfunded, deliberately dismantled and financialized, no such fate awaited the global financial sector, who promptly rewarded the public's world-wide display of benevolence by refusing to suspend its usual 'bonus culture'. In Bauman's own words, reflecting on the UK:

> The moment it was halted at the edge of a precipice by a lavish injection of 'taxpayers' money', TSB Lloyds bank started lobbying the Treasury to divert part of the rescue package to shareholders' dividends; notwithstanding the official indignation of state spokespersons, it proceeded undisturbed to pay bonuses to those whose intemperate greed had brought disaster on the banks and their clients.[8]

What enables such a capture of the state by the finance industry is precisely the idea that it is too complicated for the public to understand. The language used to account for the actions of financiers is obstructive to the public's ability to appreciate fully the implications of what is being done in their name through tacit support by the state. While the professional class of financiers enjoy the same privileges as those high priests of pre-modern societies, confounding their congregation by deliberately speaking a language only they understood, so too the public are left to feel the same now as they did then: as embarrassed to cough out loud in a bank as they were once fearful of the consequences of coughing out loud in church.

If the requirement to make sound financial decisions today influences to a huge degree our ability to enjoy happiness and a 'good life', and as more and more aspects of the collective safety nets once put in place by democratic states to protect their citizens from structural inequalities or individual misfortunes are being eroded and replaced with market-based alternatives with access to finance a significant barrier to entry, then our relationship to money becomes just as important as our relationship to the state in determining our life chances. As such, there is today a pressing need for a mass social movement that seeks to democratize finance in much the same way that people once campaigned to democratize our governments. Put simply, with the power over money concentrated in the hands of so few, and circulating through financial channels also to the benefit of those few, it becomes easy to see why we need to find alternative ways of putting the power over money into the hands of the many. Only in this way might money find a new way of travelling, a new destination that benefits rather more people than the present system permits.

Guardians of the financial Republic

In tracing a history of the relationship between democracy and finance, it is useful to recall the ancient Athenian philosopher Plato's description of the 'ideal state' in *Politeia* (Republic), his famous Socratic dialogue on the nature of justice, the soul and the state.[9] In doing so, we can recognize many of the contemporary justifications for placing our wealth in 'trust' to the finance industry. To trust in a higher power, according to Plato, was rooted in a distrust of the appetites of our soul, especially when it comes to money. This distrust of individual motives when it comes to financial decisions provides much of the justification for the continued social licence afforded to the experts of the finance industry, and so also serves to legitimate the economic fees and 'rents' extracted from that privileged position of trust.[10]

The ideal state of governance described by Plato, which takes the form of the creation of trusted Philosopher Guardians of 'the good', is equally recognizable in the narrative of public service favoured by the governors of the Bank of England who frequently sidestep issues of their own financial motives. Consider the following exchange during Mark Carney's second lecture in the 2020 Reith series for the BBC:

> Professor McCloskey: Yes, well, if it were easy to smooth things, you and I could make an unlimited fortune. There is an American proverb that applies, "If you're so smart, why aren't you rich?".

Dr Carney: You don't get rich in public service, Dierdre. You don't want – well – well, some do but that's not – that's not – not in our – our world.

Anita Anand: That is interesting. Actually, I was talking to somebody who knows you rather well who said, "It's very strange about Mark Carney, as a man who has been such a powerful banker, he has very little interest in money", and that seems to be what you've just – you've just said yourself.[11]

Just as Carney claims that he would have made a lot more money working within the system, as opposed to looking after it, Plato too insisted that the ruling class of an 'ideal state' must be neutral when it comes to their needs regarding money and the urge to increase wealth. Understanding how and why these ideas continue to shape the stories and myths about money and finance, despite the societies they are meant to serve being so unrecognizable in their complexity and scale from Plato's time, also played an important role in shaping the nascent crowdfunding and P2P finance movements.

If this seems a rather hypothetical example, it is worth noting that in January 2020 the Italian president invited the ex-governor of the European Central Bank (ECB), 'Super Mario' Draghi, to form a government. This decision was taken in the light of an enduring democratic crisis in the country resulting in a distinct polarization of Italian politics during the previous decades, and further buffeted in the short term by the acute impact there of the COVID-19 pandemic. This strategy has been used before, of course. In 2011, Mario Monti (also a former central banker) was likewise called upon by the Italian government to manage the country in the aftermath of the global crash of 2008. What both examples reveal is a growing acceptance of technocracy over democracy, the only question raised being which economist or school of economics Draghi might rely upon for his political agenda. Recalling a conversation with the UK's former Chancellor of the Exchequer,

George Osborne, Mark Carney joked during the first of his 2020 Reith lectures that 'it is easier to be a central banker in a democracy than a politician'.[12] It is not clear what his views are as to the ease of a central banker becoming a politician in a democracy.

All of which sets the scene for an important question: like Plato's imagined citizens of his ideal state, why is the public seemingly so content to be ruled by these Philosopher Guardians? Are we truly to believe that they operate guided solely by the light of public service and that their judgements really are value-free and exempt of human weaknesses and misconceptions about the true nature of things? Do they really abstain from accumulating wealth and property, relying instead on a share of the productive means of the poorer classes? When Plato critiques what he sees as the five fundamental regimes of the state – these being Aristocracy, Timocracy, Oligarchy, Democracy and Tyranny – he chooses to represent those forms in terms of a state of degeneration from the ideal, corrupted by the pursuit of imperfect 'goods' such as honour, power, desires and (of course!) the thing that enables them all: *money*. The ideal that he contrasts with these 'real world' imperfections is, in his view, a literal form of 'aristocracy', namely rule by the 'best' people, understood as those with the moderate philosophical temperament to understand the ideal of the good. Each of these imperfections from the ideal are linked to a specific system of government: the excessive pursuit of honour (in war); wealth and property (oligarchy and inequality); freedom of appetites (democracy); and finally, power through tyranny, cited as the ultimate outcome of democratic anarchy according to Plato.

Most pointedly, and perhaps unsurprising given Plato's direct experience of the low point of Athenian democracy at the end of the 5th century BCE, it is 'democratic man' that is the offspring of 'oligarchic man'. The latter is a person whose combination of ambition and prudence with wealth leads to excessive accumulation that in turn seduces his son ('democratic man') to individual wastefulness. Wealth, status and power are merely 'shadows' of the ideal of what is good, tempting and corrupting those who lack the capacity in their soul to understand and internalize the ideal in their daily life. Plato does not imply this cycle of degeneration is a deterministic process. Instead, by developing a critical perspective on his own Athenian system of government, Plato begins to question the 'wisdom of the crowd' as the best way to ensure that a state is governed with a view to what is good. Within that critique, Plato sees the problem of money, and its use in lending and investment, as tempting an insatiable appetite in the soul, an object whose acquisition seems only to make its acquirer yearn for still more of that same object. As Socrates reminds one of his interlocuters in the *Republic*, it is the power of education that can impact upon the 'rational' and 'spirited' elements of the soul:

> When these two elements are brought up on a diet of this kind, when they truly receive the teaching and education appropriate to them, then the two of them will exercise rule over the appetitive element, which in any individual is the largest part of the soul, and by nature quite insatiable where money is concerned.[13]

In this respect, Plato is reflecting a wider belief that the purpose of money is circular – accumulated simply for its own sake – and as such becomes a progressively corrupting influence that 'crowds out' reason from decision-making, in spite of money's ability to be used to meet the needs of others. For Plato, it was necessary to break free from this influence without banning money and finance completely, by giving power over the state to a class of individuals who were able to rise above such weaknesses through a combination of education, regulation and philosophical training. Some 2,500 years later, 'Super Mario' Draghi, the man who would 'do what it takes' to save the Euro, demonstrates the power of this belief and how far our world has become beholden to the idea that it is only a noble ethics of public service that drives the financial system.

Almost independent of the actual policies and practices being proposed, the belief in the need for conservative values and elite individual 'guardians' to keep our relationship with money and finance 'under control' is therefore deeply rooted in Western European culture and history. Unpacking that conservatism further helps to explain why people distrust their own motives when it comes to money and often feel at best ambivalent and at worst suspicious about those systems of finance that put individuals in control of making financial decisions and assuming responsibility for their own financial well-being.

Xenophon – a soldier, essayist and a contemporary friend of Socrates – is a useful guide in understanding this ambivalence about the value of giving control over money and finance to individuals. In his treatise *Oikonomica*, or 'principles of household management', Xenophon outlines a discussion on the use of money. Focusing upon how to invest and grow wealth, he stresses the problems that arise from the 'need for money', which still resonate with readers today. Xenophon helps us to understand how the distinction between saving and investing today concerns far more than simply a different category of financial product. Rather, it represents competing and conflicting moralities that are played out everywhere from individual financial decision-making to the politics of our national budgets and spending.

Saving versus investing

At the start of the *Oikonomica*, Xenophon recalls the meeting of Socrates and his friend Critobulus, a wealthy citizen of Athens, and recounts their discussion about the nature of productive and unproductive uses of wealth. Writ large across their dialogue is the morality of saving and prudence, the conservation of wealth and value through moderation, and the practice of investment and risk that characterizes the experience of money away from the 'home' (*oikos*, hence *oiko-nomica*), which brings excesses of pleasure together with the potential for ruin. In the discussion that follows, Socrates is the champion of these conservative attitudes to money, which 'keep money at a distance' as something to be conserved and controlled. Later, according to Plato, at his trial for 'corrupting the youth and failing to respect the gods of the City', Socrates argued that he should be supported financially by the state because he himself cared more about the search for what is 'good' than he did about money. His demand for an early form of 'individual basic income' apparently did not endear him to the jurors deciding his fate.

The roots of these beliefs, which pre-date Christianity's own views on money lending, go some way to explaining why the act of 'saving' still occupies an almost sacred moral category of activity in everyday life and discourse today. Despite the connotations of hoarded wealth, the act of saving is seen as being 'prudent'. This prudence comes despite the risk that arises should everybody collectively decide that saving wealth is the best cause of action, since this would result in modern economies swiftly ceasing to function. This phenomenon was conceived in the mid-20th century by John Maynard Keynes and later popularized as the 'paradox of thrift' by Paul Anthony Samuelson and William Nordhaus.[14] Saving is a private 'good' with a public cost, and taken too far undermines the idea of prudence by collectively impoverishing society as a whole through reduced investment and spending. To compound the issue, at the same time as we moralize about the benefits of saving, we also denigrate the act of investing as being taboo, akin to gambling. That is, investing involves taking a risk with money that could result in the 'shame' of its seemingly imprudent loss.

The creation of a taboo around the practice of investment is problematic for any democratic society, since it pushes the power over investment decisions away from individuals. Investments are in reality deeply political decisions that allocate our collective financial capital to achieve and realize future goals that may or may not align with our own values. As individuals working within tightly regulated businesses, investment professionals still have enormous power over the decisions to invest our money. When we deny people the world-making power of that responsibility in the name of 'prudence', we place that power into the hands of others – whether they be an embodied professional financier, an algorithm or an index – that can lay claim to being politically neutral and driven only by the rational calculation of maximum profit. It is this line of thinking that sees market forces established as an almost natural process, independently adjudicating on the investments that ultimately shape our world, despite the evidence of Alan Greenspan, former Chair of the US Federal Reserve, pertaining to the 'fatal flaw' in the thinking that markets know best.[15]

The global trend to ensure finance is both regulated and managed 'independently' of politics and politicians has taken much of the accountability for those decisions out of the democratic realm. While the shift towards establishing a firewall between politics and central bank independence may now have reached its zenith in the political tensions between EU member states and the ECB, as highlighted by Adam Tooze, the tensions between those who seek control over financial capital (and the political power it asserts) and those who ultimately create and own the flows of value that it captures, can be seen throughout human history.[16] Money is the most powerful tool for collective action ever invented, and yet it is how we organize finance that ultimately determines who controls that power and how far that collective action serves the interests of society as a whole.

It is surprising therefore that many mainstream economists continue to treat money and finance as somehow neutral, rather than as a social construct that both shapes and is shaped by social relations, values and goals. This 'neutral' consensus means that the global regulation and management of the financial system now largely occurs independent of democratic politics, almost to the extent that such interventions constitute a taboo for democratic oversight. As we will argue in Chapter Five, the development of innovations such as crowdfunding lay bare the tensions between the very real political consequences of finance and our desire to democratize the financial system and those who govern and shape its function.

The tension in the relationship between finance and the *politeia* is revealed in the stories of the birth of democracy itself in the 6th century BCE (two hundred years before Plato's writing). The emergence of democracy as a form of government of the 'city state', or *polis*, was the product of many years of negotiation between the political classes. It first required a catalyst, however, which arrived in the shape of a radical reform of the system of finance, in particular banning enforcement of debt through human bondage, which was repealed by the reforms of Solon, Archon of Athens, also at the beginning of the 6th century BCE.[17] These reforms are cited as the start of the long process of development that led to the creation of the world's first democracy. Solon's bid to end the principle of debt bondage and possibly also the cancellation of debts between citizens (including the return of citizens in exile fleeing the punishment of slavery, which default on a debt could bring) laid the foundations for the broadening of the citizen franchise and put the Athenians on the road to what became the first democratic system of government.

Solon's reforms meant that powerful individuals, the aristocratic class of Athenian landowners, could no longer use their financial resources as a means to assert control over less well-off citizens, who had to borrow money due to the impact of unexpected weather events, poor harvests, warfare and so on, which created further stress for those whose landholdings and labour provided sufficient subsistence only if things went well. Default on those debts allowed the lenders to assert obligations on the debtor which effectively placed either the individual or members of his *oikos* into debt bondage. A succession of such events therefore dramatically concentrated both power and wealth among the elite who had the resources to weather the storms and to finance increasingly aggressive and ultimately damaging competition between elite individuals for power within the state itself. These tensions were also exploited by a succession of populist tyrants whom the final democratic revolution successfully overthrew.

As the various Greek city-states began to look beyond their borders for both trade and acquisition of territory, so they became increasingly reliant on being able to call upon a body of men to defend or assert those claims. As is often the case in history, it was the sacrifice of war that drove a political desire for greater enfranchisement and rights as citizens, of which protection from the ultimate sanctions of financial debt were an important addition.

P2P finance, a 2,500-year-old new idea

After half a century or more of relative stability since the Second World War, Zygmunt Bauman argued that the once 'solid' modern institutions that governed society are today in the process of dissolving into a state of 'liquidity', where almost nothing is stable and everything seems to change without warning. As we saw in Chapter One, Bauman described this as a period of *interregnum*, during which societies either have to develop new social structures capable of responding to the grand challenges of the new century or else create more nimble systems and lifestyles to cope with the now permanent uncertainties and acute anxieties of daily life in what he described as 'liquid modernity'.[18]

The present situation thus shares similarities with the interregnum in Athens and other Hellenic city-states during the time of Solon and later the enigmatic creator of democracy, Kleisthenes. Out of that period of interregnum, the Athenian model of democracy was created on the basis of emerging ideas of individual freedom and, more importantly for the ancient Greeks, *isonomia* (or 'equality before the law'), running counter to the centuries-old traditions of rule 'by the best' (aristocracy). To move beyond our current period of interregnum, we argue that a similar renegotiation of the relationship between democracy and finance must be settled in favour of people and planet. In striving to achieve this, there are important lessons to be learned from a more thorough consideration of how that settlement has been negotiated in the past and how it has already shaped the development of alternative finance.

To examine crowdfunding and P2P finance through ancient historical sources provides a fresh context through which to view the relationship between democracy and finance. In particular, the work of Paul Millett – that also played an influential role in the development of the P2P finance platform Zopa, alongside the work of Zygmunt Bauman – offers a fascinating analysis of a long forgotten social life of money that inspired the first democratic society and signals the importance of finance in that process.[19] As Millett sets out in the frontispiece of his book:

Lending and borrowing were commonplace in Athens during the 4th Century BC and could involve interest rates, security and banks, but the part played by credit was very different from its familiar role in capitalist society today … lending and borrowing were a way of *ordering social relations* between Athenian citizens.

Although debt could be disruptive, it had as its more positive side, the strengthening of ties between individuals. That was, in turn, an aspect of the solidarity between citizens which was a part of the Athenian democracy.[20]

The role of finance in 'ordering social relations' means that we have to take seriously the purpose of finance – the social and environment outcomes it produces and thus its very real legacy for humankind and the rest of the planet – over and above our obsession with its technical function. Indeed, what is striking about the descriptions of different ancient forms of commonplace lending and borrowing that can be gleaned from Millett's analysis are the ways in which debt – far from being the disruptive social force intended to be addressed by the reforms of Solon – was in fact part of how the citizen body coped with unexpected costs or financial stress. As the anthropologist and activist David Graeber also showed in his equally magisterial study of finance in the period,[21] debt was how citizens met their social and religious obligations as a community, what Aristotle characterized in his book *Politics* as *koinoneia*, which loosely translates as 'community of interests'.

We argue that debt has always had an important role to play in forming and sustaining this 'reciprocity' between citizens. While conventional economic thinking would see reciprocity as potential 'interference' in the process of deciding value, it is one-sided to overlook the anthropological studies that show how debt has been used throughout human history also to form broader community or altruistic interests between people. Viewed from this historical perspective, we are left to conclude that our prejudice against the concept of debt in society, often characterized as an 'ill', is peculiar to our time and place in history. What sociologists are right to highlight is the exploitative tendencies of different types of debt relations, but such exploitation is not a given. Debt markets can have moral motivations. This is exactly the problem that Mark Carney lamented as the 'drift from moral to market sentiments' in his opening 2020 Reith lecture.

The important question, then, is not about the suitability or otherwise of debt as a basis for democratic financial relationships. What matters are the ways in which systems of finance are sanctioned to enforce agreements at the expense of wider political principles of individual freedom, citizenship and equality before the law. Crucially for our argument here, Millett helps us to look beyond the value of a financial system as being simply a matter of its function – such as its role in creating liquidity, efficiency and so on – to one that instead examines its wider purpose and value to society. This idea is a clear challenge to the modern belief that the only purpose of finance is simply to invest money to generate more money, and that such a service is intrinsically useful and valuable to society. Millett offers us a window onto an ancient society that seemed tacitly to recognize the role of finance in creating social value through reciprocity, not destroying it.

The specific inspiration of P2P finance was a system described by Millett and others as an *eranos* loan. The etymology of *eranos* in ancient Greek derives from the concept of a shared meal, where everyone would bring a small contribution (known elsewhere as 'potlatch'). This idea of everyone contributing a small portion, in order to build up sufficient food to satiate the needs of everyone, is obviously also a founding principle of crowdfunding. Millett provides evidence of how *eranos* loans were commonplace in the social life of money in democratic Athens and how they played a role in maintaining the cohesion of that political system. In Millett's view, these informal community-based schemes evolved with the growth in size and complexity of the Athenian state to allow transactions not only between kinship groups and village communities, but also with far larger metropolitan and suburban populations with whom people held weaker social connections.

Eranos loans did not incur any interest, but they did carry the expectation of a return of the favour should the need arise at a later date. The obligation was enforced informally by the norms and values of people themselves. Refusing to help someone who made such an entreaty was often used in the law courts as evidence of a plaintiff's or a defendant's bad character. *Eranos* loans could be arranged as a 'one-to-one' direct arrangement, or as more elaborate 'one-to-many' arrangements just like today, with the seminal difference being the absence of interest accrued. In their own ways, both Millett and Graeber make the insightful point that, by establishing a system of interest payments accrued alongside the loan, social obligations between people are swiftly cancelled once the loan plus interest amount is settled. The system removed any future obligation on the part of the borrower to return the favour, thus using debt to close off and cancel social relations rather than to sustain a web of mutual interdependence between them.

Millett finds further evidence of this understanding of the social life of money in the poems of Hesiod (c. 750–650 BCE). 'Works and Days' provides particular insights into the life of peasant farmers at the time, as well as anthropological accounts of attitudes towards subsistence farmers today in Mexico. Millett draws on G.M. Foster to unpick the apparent contradictions within the writings of Hesiod between the idea of self-reliance and good neighbourliness with his description of the ideal of success as:

> to be able to live *sin compromisos*, to be strong, masculine, independent, able to meet life's continuing challenges without help from others, to be able to avoid entangling alliances. Yet, paradoxically, the struggle to reach this goal can only be made by saddling oneself with a wide variety of obligations. Strength and independence in fact always depend on the number and quality of the ties one maintains.[22]

The idea that independence and self-reliance require a vital network of favours and obligations upon which individuals are able to ride out the bad times and support others in the good is well-known in sociology and anthropology. To stay with our example of farming, it is what ensures that should one's neighbour suffer the loss of a crop to a hailstorm or flood, while your side of the valley remains relatively unscathed, there is a way of you both surviving.

The realization that money and finance themselves are simple social constructs, built from the values and aspirations of the society from which they emerge and for whom they are meant to serve, influenced the innovators of crowdfunding and P2P lending to find new ways to ensure that process was derived from democratic forms of decision-making and deliberation. Rather than disciplining democratic motives, the aim of the alternative finance movement was explicitly to bring those motives back into finance. In effect, there was an urgent need to create new systems of trust that could reverse that drift from 'moral' to 'market' sentiments in finance. Democratizing finance then becomes not merely a populist project of 'taking back control' of money, but a more transformational moment that seeks to navigate a way out of the present interregnum by deploying all of the mechanisms of democracy to ensure that money, and the financial system that is built upon it, is imbued with social values and so seeks to create a world where people and planet are not treated coldly as mere externalities in a crude calculation of profit and loss.

Our point here is radically against the wisdom of the moment, where the guiding principle of central bankers around the world is to ensure precisely the opposite: that the financial system is as liberated and as independent as possible from the interference of other people in its operations and functions. What underpins this view of central bankers is, in part at least, an affinity with Plato's cynicism about the wisdom of the crowd as already noted. More specifically, how finance (positively in their view) 'crowds out' the values which individuals share and instead emphasizes selfish motivations. Any attempt to 'crowd in' the values, motivations and aspirations of the people can thus only be seen as disrupting the function of a finance system that can only operate when such social justice 'impurities' are cleansed from it.

This is the fundamental challenge of crowdfunding, which facilitates a democratization of investment but does not necessarily solve the problem of 'who decides' upon the best use of money in society. Democracy, as Plato and the central bankers would surely both contend, risks citizens becoming vulnerable to the blandishments of rhetoric and the empty promises of demagogues, ultimately replacing the tyranny of the individual with the tyranny of the majority. And yet, looking around the world today at the grand challenges facing all people of the planet, and when the survival of both is truly at stake, can it really be credible to argue still that a few enlightened financiers are better at deciding upon the best use of money? Should people themselves not be 'crowded in' to have more of a say on those financial matters that concern them all?

Digging for coins

There is a risk that in digging through the history of money, all you find are coins. The arguments rehearsed throughout this chapter have aimed to underlie a set of different prescriptions for a better finance system, prescriptions that are reflected in ancient societies with a different political settlement between democracy and finance. Through Millett, Graeber and others, what we find is a need for a more pluralistic and flexible approach to understanding how different forms of money and finance have been both novated and innovated over time with the ebb and flow of human cultures and societies. Even a cursory review of the 'social life of money' shows that not only do moralities and practices of money change over time, but that they can also co-exist within a single nation or society.

The last of our Greek witnesses to money is the Athenian comic playwright Aristophanes, another contemporary of Socrates, who made these conflicts the target of his satire by penning a play called *Plutus*. Plutus or 'Wealth' is brought to life as a god so as to hold a mirror to the Athenian audience's views on money, finance and the accumulation of wealth. The fallen god suffers many woes, from being buried in the ground (by the miser) to being flung at expensive courtesans (by the profligate spender), blinded by Zeus such that the gifts of wealth are distributed by luck rather than by judgement. His sight restored by a visit to the god of healing, Plutus begins to distribute wealth to the deserving and importantly sets about depriving the undeserving. In the end, this brings down the reign of Zeus himself as Plutus replaces the king of the gods as the object of human prayers. Aristophanes seeks his satirical humour in this world turned upside down, but at the same time makes a more subtle point about the nature of wealth and how it underpins the hierarchy of the world as we know it.

The powerful belief that 'good money' is somehow solid and enduring, value that is to be conserved and stored, whereas 'bad money' can disappear as quickly as it appears, has distorted our view of the past when studying the growth and development of financial institutions. Banking, investment, credit and payment are functions that we expect to recognize in any study of the past. This belief is no different when we think about money itself, which for most people is an embodied or material concept, namely cash in the form of notes and coins. Many continue to seek the roots of money in the numismatic study of coins as providing solid evidence for the permanence of money's existence throughout human history. This desire for solidity, for something rooted, and a value that is materially 'real' can, like Zeus, blind us to the fundamental linkages and tensions between finance and society, money and politics.

What is recognizable in this historical inquiry is just how much the apparent solidity of money is based upon little more than the power of the human imagination and the need to build social bonds of trust and reciprocity to survive in an uncertain and ever-changing world. The different (and similar) historical meanings of money and finance are therefore of more than only academic interest. Looking to the past can help to support the creation of new and innovative ways of thinking about money that in turn begin to develop new forms of financial co-operation intended to meet the grand challenges of the present day. Finance reflects the politics of our world and, if we are to follow the principles of democracy and come together as citizens to meet those challenges, then we need to find ways that our democratic will can be expressed through finance.

One of the most visionary scholars of money and finance working today, Keith Hart, frames this problem in terms of the 'two sides of a coin'.[23] The 'head' represents the power of the state, which enables money to exist and provides the basis for the systems of trust upon which its apparent 'solidity' is built. On the reverse, the 'tails' denotes the more 'liquid' systems of market exchange and negotiation, which enable individuals to meet their needs and leverage their capital to create future streams of value. Hart's insight is important because, despite the upheavals and crises of the last four decades of neoliberal financialization, the institutions of finance still claim a great deal of their legitimacy from longevity and the image of unalterable permanence. Banking in particular prides itself on securing permanence and solidity while avoiding change and fluidity, with nations competing to claim the oldest 'continuous' bank in existence.

As bank customers, therefore, we also want to believe in this idea of permanence and resilience, and we can be shaken when those beliefs are challenged by experience. In 2008, it was the pictures on UK national television news of people queuing outside of the Northern Rock bank branch in the genteel suburban town of Kingston upon Thames that brought home the urgency of the first stages of the global crash, far more so than any technical understanding of that organization's reliance upon the short-term money markets to fund its lending. This long-held reverence for the safety of a bank as an institution contrasts sharply with how comfortable people seem to be today about dining out and drinking in now defunct bank branches, or drinking coffee on what used to be stock exchange floors. Of course, the irony here is that an actual bank branch does not 'contain' any money of its own beyond its daily float (provided by the Bank of England in the form of notes and coins).

From Goschen loans to Community Municipal Investments

In his book *The National Debt*, Martin Slater narrates the role of debt in the political formation of the United Kingdom, specifically through its wars, its colonial empires and, in the 20th century, its varied attempts to 'pay back' that debt.[24] Slater's fascinating story puts another intriguing character centre stage, namely the UK's National Savings, which until the latter half of the 20th century were one of the main sources of funds for government borrowing. Indeed, whereas today those engaged in the stock market are more likely to be pursuing company equity investments, prior to the 1920s stocks were made up mainly of government and corporate bonds.

Slater's account is rich in both technical and historical detail, painting a picture of the changing fortunes of the UK's national debt and the changing attitudes of the general public and subsequent generations of Chancellors of the Exchequer towards even the idea of a national debt. Slater recalls how it provided the means for a weaker nation in terms of land and population to finance a succession of wars with stronger nations, by borrowing over the long term (sometimes in perpetuity) to finance the short-term expenditure necessary. In times of peace, the uses of debt shifted from swords to ploughshares and was used to finance much of the public infrastructure that we take for granted today.

Although not the first to do so, the Bank of England was certainly the most successful lender to the government, establishing itself under a charter as a Limited Joint Stock Company in 1694 with a loan of £1.2 million that paid 8 per cent interest in perpetuity.[25] The security of this income allowed the bank to issue its own bonds via an early form of P2P finance ('marketplace lending'). The enabler of this innovation was a change in 1690 following the Glorious Revolution which gave parliament rather than the Crown control over the creation of money. Trust in the prudence of democracy, rather than being at the behest of the capricious whims of more or less tyrannical monarchs, was challenged and lampooned by conservative cartoonists just as acerbically as today. The Bank of England made many more loans this way, as each war fought effectively doubled the national debt until it reached £893 million at the end of the Napoleonic wars. This total represented around 200 per cent of estimated gross domestic product (GDP), a level it would not reach again until the rebuilding of the nation after the Second World War. To fund that effort, it was citizens themselves as much as Threadneedle Street that became a main source of capital for the government's recovery at home and expansion throughout its colonial empire.[26]

Throughout this time, Chancellors of the Exchequer made or unmade their reputations based upon schemes to repay the national debt. A leading Liberal prime minister at different points throughout the latter half of the 19th century, William Gladstone in particular stands out for his long-standing role at the centre of the nation's finances. Gladstone's legacy endured beyond his tenures of office by advocating for a mix of laissez-faire economics with a strong conservative instinct to 'pay off' the nation's debts. These principles of so-called 'prudent' public finance built upon Gladstone's private moralities of debt and is a familiar theme at the time of writing, as nations grapple with the huge increases in government spending prompted by the COVID-19 pandemic and are currently faced with a genuine crisis: deciding how that spending should be accounted for on the national balance sheet.

In Gladstone's time, much of the national debt was held by the middle class of the home nation, often in the form of long-term *consols* (an abbreviation of 'consolidated bonds'), which were low interest, long-term securities issued during times of peace in order to refinance the more expensive short-term borrowing of war. In reality, as Slater illustrates, the national debt was made up of the deposits from the nation's savings.

Even though no *consols* were issued after 1927, the last one was not repaid until 2015 when historically low interest rates caused by the Bank of England's monetary policy, and in particular the practice of QE as a response to the 2008 global crash, made it convenient to repay the perpetual debt on the government's books.

The role of citizens in raising and earning a return from government debt has exercised the minds of many Chancellors, including the current incumbent in 2021, Rishi Sunak. His 2017 paper, before he was elevated to the Treasury, argued strongly for the benefits of issuing bonds to boost the relatively under-capitalized state of the UK's small businesses by appealing to small investors.[27] But it isn't only in times of peace that the government has turned to citizens essentially to crowdfund its borrowing. During both World Wars, billions of pounds were raised by government 'war bonds' to fund the effort at home and overseas.

Although the amounts raised seem small relative to today's National Savings balance, the principle that bond structures could be utilized to enable citizens collectively to invest for a common purpose is an important historical precedent for the argument we are making here. Crowdfunding and P2P finance provide an alternative way of moving money such that it can be given or invested to projects and causes that people collectively care about, from the survival of the nation state during times of war through to saving the planet by supporting projects that help to transition societies fairly to net zero. In this way, a healthier relationship between democracy and finance can be fostered through crowdfunding by ensuring money is put directly into the service of those values of reciprocity and community that are so vital to a cohesive society. Furthermore, crowdfunding helps us to address in part the problem of 'who decides' where and how money is invested. Refusing to grant that power to a professional class of mainstream economists and financiers, who claim to know more and to merit our trust, crowdfunding and P2P finance put citizens in charge of what money does and offer the opportunity to build a far better world than the current financial system appears capable of delivering.

And the role of bonds in providing a form of finance for society is currently being rediscovered. At the national level, the UK government's budget statement in March 2021 included a welcome commitment to a new 'green bonds' saving structure to be offered to retail investors, as well as the Bank of England itself being given a new monetary policy directive aligned to achieving net zero targets. For our part, we have applied the insights contained in this book to create a new investment-based crowdfunding structure known as CMIs.[28] A form of crowdfunded public debt underwritten by local governments, CMIs are a new model of lending that draws inspiration from the 1880s. In between Gladstone's several tenures of office as prime minister, then Chancellor of the Exchequer, 1st Viscount George Joachim Goschen essentially crowdfunded more than £400 million of local authority loans through the Post Office (around £53 billion in today's money). The proceeds funded the investments of local entrepreneurs and their municipal corporations, which at the time were building the UK's major cities. Known as 'Goschen loans', this practice continued in the form of municipal bonds until the early 1990s when, just before the internet arrived, the administrative cost of what were then burdensome paper-based processes finally proved too inefficient for councils to afford. Now reinvented for the internet-enabled investment world, CMIs were developed through research with six UK public sector case studies throughout 2018–19. In the summer of 2020, the UK's first CMIs were launched by two councils, West Berkshire and Warrington, raising £2 million for local net-zero projects. In July 2021, CMIs became part of a UK-wide campaign led by the Green Finance Institute to promote local climate bonds.

Central to the thinking behind CMIs was the concept of public or civic investment and the realization that finance can be used to create both social and economic value. It is a political decision, after all, to prioritize the latter only. Just as the system of *eranos* loans in ancient Athens contributed to the solidarity and community of the citizen body, so vital for the discipline of the phalanx and the trireme during times of war, so crowdfunding investments in our social and economic infrastructure today remind us of the ties that bind us and how our very survival rests upon a recognition of our interdependence upon each other. The development of CMIs shows that we need to move beyond the idea that money and finance are built around the resilience and prosperity of the private individual, and instead reconnect finance with democracy by finding new ways of investing in the public sphere. At least a part of the reason why people find it so hard to direct our money to the greater purpose of tackling the current and oncoming crises of COVID-19, Climate and Care – to refocus Carney's triple threat more onto the needs of humanity, rather than finance – is the enduring misconception that somehow any money spent in the public sphere has been 'pinched' from private pockets.[29]

This is why we are arguing that the democratization of finance is so important. Taking control of money, and the wider finance system, through democratic means is no different to taking control of the other levers of state power. Our claim here is that there is no such thing as 'passive investment'. In reality, such passivity is simply the abdication of personal responsibility for the value of your money to society as a whole. The financial decisions you are making right now are impacting the world around you, whether you know that or not. The study of the relationship between democracy and finance in the past is a helpful reminder of the myths and stories that have shaped and continue to shape the beliefs and practices of today's financial system.

The development of CMIs is an attempt to reverse the trend for crowdfunding and P2P finance to be absorbed into the mainstream comfort zone of money as usual, moving away from trusting individual professional decision-makers and supporting collective action with our money to re-write the narrative around the value of savings for social or national goals, and break the stranglehold that the private financial sector has on the destination of money.

FOUR

The Destination of Money

In February 2021, Marie Ekeland, one of the most influential figures in the French FinTech sector, set out the ambition for her new funding vehicle *2050* – designed to have a long-term positive impact on issues like equality and sustainability – in the following way:

> When you invest, you're shaping the future. When you put your money here, you're not just following the wind, you're making it blow. So the real question is: 'What is the world you want to live in?' This question is very complex to answer because we're living in a very complex world and there is no vision that is well articulated today.[1]

In the absence of an overarching and positive vision of how to build a better world collectively through formal democratic processes, and with the future appearing to promise little more than an endless series of world-ending threats to be managed in order to mitigate their most harmful effects, Ekeland struck a more optimistic note in the same article with a very simple but profound observation: 'Money is actually very powerful but it has to have a destination … If finance is only reproducing the past, then we're not going to find any solutions to the current new challenges that we have because people do not know how to solve them.'

The story that finance likes to tell about itself, at least since the entrepreneurial turn of the 1980s, is that it is at the cutting edge of innovation. It is certainly true that the plethora of new financial products that have emerged onto the market, especially since the internet revolution of the 2000s, have become increasingly complex and fantastical in their ability to evade popular understanding and thus any real democratic accountability. But what is striking about Ekeland's observation from the very epicentre of the financial innovation sector is how little all of this Promethean creativity has contributed to the betterment of society. Indeed, by 'only reproducing the past', finance for all its innovation has too often simply maintained the injustices of the status quo. Far from the radical liberator that appears in fairy tales told by and about the sector, mainstream financial innovation has largely exaggerated and entrenched existing inequalities and had a devastating impact on the natural environment.

And there is a clue within Ekeland's remarks as to why this is so. Finance, and the economic models that serve to legitimate its functions, has either lost or never really developed any sense of purpose. If not for the betterment of society, we might ask: what is finance, and especially financial innovation, for? In her book *Mission Economy*, Mariana Mazzucato captures this problematic with characteristic precision when she explains that the problem with finance today is that it is being used largely to finance itself, not society. Most finance, she continues, simply goes back into finance, insurance and real estate (which she expresses with the acronym FIRE), and is almost never used to invest in the productive economy.[2] In Ekeland's terms, the problem here is that money's destination is money.

Almost the entire architecture of today's financial system is designed and governed in such a way that money's ultimate and only destination is to generate more of itself for those who already had it in the first place. This situation has significant consequences for rising levels of inequality. The fixed costs of managing money are usually generated in terms of the individual customer. The amount of money that a customer has does not significantly increase those fixed costs but adds only a small marginal cost. The finance industry, therefore, focuses primarily upon ways to help those people who already have lots of money to preserve (or in more sociological terms, to *reproduce*) their position in the social hierarchy by giving them a more privileged access to both financial and real assets whose returns (as Piketty and others have analysed) are greater than both wages and inflation.[3]

All of which brings us to a significant moment for our argument in this book. We propose that what needs to be innovated is less the technical functions of how finance operates – the complex and often algorithmically driven products and systems of finance – and instead, the imagination of finance urgently needs to rediscover its purpose, its sense of societal mission. In moving through a relatively closed loop of FIRE investments, the world that finance appears to want to live in is one of social and environmental degradation. What Mark Carney called 'the tragedy of the horizon' is often taken to mean the short-termism of the City and its culture of 'profit now, pay later'.[4] In truth, the tragedy is not only about greed but, as we saw in Chapter Three, rather the pursuit of what is termed 'prudence' (financial stability) no matter what the cost to people and planet.[5] At present, the only mission of finance appears to be its own reproduction, with the (social, environmental, well-being) costs of finance held strictly 'off balance sheet' as mere externalities never fully accounted for in the final reckoning (at least, until now).

What finance does not appear to see, perhaps because in creating and administering these financial circuits it thinks too rarely about money's destination, is its own direct role in delivering those deleterious outcomes. From the cohesion of society beginning to break down due to rising levels of inequality, through to anti-democratic tendencies emerging through a widespread loss of trust in the way the entire social system operates, these are not random external events to which the models of finance simply have to respond. Societal breakdown is in part a direct consequence of how those models are being allowed to operate with too little democratic oversight and so too little accountability to the public.

In seeking to explore whether crowdfunding provides a new template for thinking about how finance serves society, and how money enables our collective purpose and individual aspirations for the future, we need to focus far less on what money *is* and devote our efforts more fully to understanding what money *does*. It is precisely because money is so powerful – as we stated at the outset, the most powerful tool for social change ever invented by human societies – that we need to think more carefully about its destination and help finance to rediscover its sense of purpose. That process, of reconnecting finance with a social and environmental mission, is what we believe to be underway in the maturing crowdfunding and P2P sectors around the world.

In this chapter, we go beyond the narrowly functional analysis of money to be found within mainstream economics teaching by shining a new light on the question of money illuminated by both sociology and anthropology, in order to provide alternative narratives about the nature of money and finance and their social legitimacy. By revealing new ways of seeing money, we raise important questions about what the destination of money ought to be and who – beyond those financial elites currently doing so – should get to decide. In the process, we will begin to see how our common beliefs about money are barriers to change and realizing positive, meaningful innovation in finance. The final section of this chapter will examine the contradictions of those beliefs and suggest ways in which those seeking progressive change in the finance system can avoid falling into the trap whereby every proposal is met with the rebuke, 'but you're not talking about real money'. The four biggest misconceptions we have about 'real money' are as follows:

First, that 'real money' is *universal*. In other words, one person's concept of money is the same as another's, and money is the same no matter where it comes from or what it is used for.

Second, that 'real money' is an *invention of reason*. This is what enables transactions to be pure calculations of 'economic' utility and objective value, and not sullied by 'social' or 'political' value(s). Before there was money, we are frequently told, the value of things was only ever negotiated through 'truck and barter' (a myth we dispelled in Chapter Three).

Third, that 'real money' is *created by work done*, or in return for 'proof of work'. Only time devoted to labour can create value, which can then be traded with others. The more work that is done, or the companies that create work, then the more money there is to go around. Connected to this idea is the misconception that money is somehow backed by something real, material and precious (such as gold). Anything else is dismissed as 'funny money'.

Fourth and final, the misconception that 'real money' must be *handled prudently because it is finite*. Our perceptions of risk, and actions taken to mitigate risk, are thus taken to be a product of individual calculations of gain and loss of a finite resource, and not governed by societal norms that may only foolishly fritter away what is left of 'real money'.

These four misconceptions mean that people are often confused when sociologists and anthropologists describe and theorize about money and finance, because in doing so they reveal the essential contradictions and dissonance that exists between our beliefs about the value of 'real money' versus the reality of money as it actually exists and is used in the world – what we have called 'the social life of money'. We can't expect the democratization of finance to have any meaningful impact if we cannot overcome the essential conservatism of our beliefs about money. It is these beliefs that have helped finance to become a system akin to a 'gilded cage' and that is thwarting the ability of society collectively to respond to the challenges we face in the 21st century.

Flat, colourless and heartless

In the aftermath of the 2008 crisis, the economist Ha-Joon Chang offered the following rallying cry: 'It is time that we dispensed with the myth that the market is a force of nature that should not be meddled with. Markets are social creations that can be, and have been, modified for social purposes.'[6] We agree and, as an academic and a practitioner, we have looked elsewhere for inspiration in asking apparently 'economic' questions. In part, this is because most major courses in economics, and (with notable exceptions) most economists themselves, focus their study of money on something very narrow and technical. So far as it occurs at all, studying money in mainstream economics courses operates in the same way that, say, the study of physics provides a meaningful analysis of football, or studying the rules of grammar and syntax reveals all we need to know about Margaret Atwood's writing. Economics basically attempts to solidify a concept that is actually far more liquid than its orthodox models permit.

To be clear, we do not mean 'liquid' here in the narrowly economic sense of being a 'readily realizable asset'. Instead, we mean 'liquid' in the sense set out in the sociology of Zygmunt Bauman, which has been guiding us throughout this book. This is because money's ephemeral nature, being a complex social system of trust, means that we need to resist attempts to reduce its meaning to this or that simplified and apparently 'solid' definition. The problem for economics is that, like all other social and cultural phenomenon, money is messy. Far from being logical and rational, our understanding and behaviours when it comes to using money, particularly when making investments, can be seen as riddled with contradictions and irrational beliefs if judged against a behavioural model that presumes rational action as the norm. This is problematic for a field of enquiry that has long stressed the scientific side of its social science status, priding itself on being able to ape the natural sciences by mathematically modelling complex phenomenon such as markets, firms or fiscal policies.

And yet, as Mary Mellor succinctly puts it: 'The "moneyness" of money reflects the trust people have in it, not the form and structure of the money itself.'[7] In a similar vein, we apply

Bauman's notion of 'liquidity' to signal that money can be all kinds of things to people in different contexts – and has been throughout human history – such that the very idea of one fixed and universal *meaning* of money is part of the reason why economists appear to find it unworthy of deeper study, and thus why so many myths about money endure to this day.

In their attempts to 'solidify' the meaning of money, mainstream economists base their analyses on a set of basic functions that money is observed to perform. Consequently, money is typically described as possessing three, four or sometimes all five of these principal utilities: a measure of value; a means of exchange; a store of wealth; a unit of account; and, more familiarly, a means of payment. In this, mainstream economics teaching treats money in a profoundly reductionist way. The debate (such as it is) about the essence and value of money reflects a tendency within Anglophone analytical philosophy to follow the doctrines of logical positivism and thus, *qua* Ludwig Wittgenstein, to limit the scope of the field of enquiry to 'things which can be defined in a sufficiently clear manner'.[8] It is this narrow focus that has motivated sufficient numbers of university economics students to demand changes to their curriculums, as expressed most powerfully by the global *Rethinking Economics* movement and the *Econocracy* book it inspired.[9] We argue that this reductionist doctrine, despite being based on a belief that to be a science we should only deal with the 'facts of the matter', plays a significant role in the inertia that is inherent within the financial system and the resistance to changes that are perceived to be motivated by social or political rather than 'pure' economic outcomes. Politics, so the belief goes, makes for bad economics, which is evidently a disavowal of the idea that economics is itself highly political.

Throughout the mainstream history of sociology, however, money too was seen in narrow, utilitarian terms. Classical 'Western' sociology, as somewhat erroneously represented by the grand figures of Max Weber (1864–1920), Karl Marx (1818–83) and Georg Simmel (1858–1918), argued in various ways that money serves to establish a universal basis for rendering everything in the human-made world *equivalent*. These thinkers became deeply worried when observing the mass transformations of industrialization, urbanization and rationalization at different stages in the development of 19th- and early 20th-century modern European societies. Money itself was seen as part of these wider social processes whereby an ever-expanding market economy began to colonize more and more social space. In his treatise *The Economic Ethics of the World Religions*, for example, Max Weber expressed his profound reservations about the creeping instrumental rationality of modern life by famously declaring that money was the 'most abstract and "impersonal" element that exists in human life'.[10]

Karl Marx had less to say on money than might be first assumed, given his status as the leading sociological analyst of capitalist political economy. Compared to the depth and breadth of his canon, Marx produced only intermittent writings on money, which he called a 'god of commodities' due to its capacity to obliterate all subjective connections between people and things by reducing personal relations to the cash nexus, characterizing it as decidedly 'anti' social. In both *Capital* and *A Contribution to the Critique of Political Economy*, the perverted processes by which social relations between people are transformed into material relations between things, according to Marx, peaks with money. Money turns all objects – whether useful, honorific or sacred – into ordinary commodities to be exchange via money's 'equation of the incompatible'.[11]

Georg Simmel's contribution to the sociological understanding of money has been far greater but has suffered a similar fate to Mark Carney's depiction of Adam Smith's book, *The Wealth of Nations*. Simmel's masterpiece, *The Philosophy of Money*, also suffers from being one of the most widely quoted and, at the same time, perhaps least read books in classical sociology. Across its 600 pages or more, Simmel paints *fin de siècle* modern societies in an 'evenly flat and grey tone', which he argues is largely thanks to money's inherent 'colourlessness', turning the entire world of human cultures into little more than a 'problem of arithmetic'. For Simmel, 'the complete heartlessness of money is reflected in our social culture, which is itself determined by money'. In other words, all of the meaningful nuances of cultural life are stamped out by a new quantitative logic of money that destroys social bonds with its brutally materialist concerns, leaving the world 'cold, distant and calculating'. Carney and Simmel thus share a similar concern, namely that social bonds and reciprocity are vital to social cohesion, and that the social licence of finance must be based on its capacity to enhance reciprocity rather than to destroy it.[12]

Money's 'uncompromising objectivity', Simmel argued, freed from its subjective restrictions and indifferent to 'particular interests, origins, or relations', ensures that the very essence of money is its 'unconditional interchangeability, the internal uniformity that makes each piece exchangeable for another'. For Simmel, money possesses a deeply troubling quality whereby, because of its capacity to quantify meaningful social relationships through the application of numbers – as in, the process of exchange between strangers, or the necessity to repay one's debts – then far from creating new and reciprocal social bonds between people, money sets a limit at which point it is possible to cancel those bonds completely.

Money neutralizes social obligations, the very basis of sociality itself, and thus begins to create an indifferent world where the modern *blasé* attitude is not only affected towards the world of cultural objects, but towards other human beings too. We are left with a society of individuals (to borrow Norbert Elias's phrase from his extension of these ideas), which almost a hundred years later would be a sentiment echoed by Margaret Thatcher at the dawn of the neoliberal age, namely that 'there is no such thing as society, only families and individuals'. More pertinently still for our argument here, it is worth recalling Thatcher's infamous 1983 speech to the Conservative Party Conference:

> Let us never forget this fundamental truth: the State has no source of money other than money which people earn themselves. If the State wishes to spend more it can do so only by borrowing your savings or by taxing you more. It is no good thinking that someone else will pay – that 'someone else' is you. There is no such thing as public money; there is only taxpayers' money.[13]

This dictum continues to dominate both the public and political understanding of money almost 40 years later. Thatcher made much of her upbringing as the daughter of a grocer and how this ensured she understood the value of 'real money'. Thatcher was thus particularly susceptible to the four misconceptions of money that we outlined in the first section of this chapter, and, as a consequence, the development of the UK's financial system has been tied up in the idea of that particular grocer's apron strings ever since.

Taking the classical economic and sociological perspectives together, we argue against the view of money that emerges from their analyses. As we have outlined in previous chapters, for a system based on and created by trust, we seemingly fail to trust ourselves when it comes to managing money. Both perspectives fail to penetrate the veil of money's neutrality and truly examine the complex and messy foundations upon which our beliefs about money are built. Rather than pursuing the logical positivist approach of trying to come up with ever more acute and 'solid' definitions of money to compete with those already established in the field of mainstream economics, more contemporary sociological and anthropological thinkers argue that money is – in our framing – 'liquid', that is, deeply qualitative. By adopting more ethnographic methods of 'deep hanging out' we are provided with 'rich descriptions' of money that are simultaneously jarring and enlightening for those who claim to understand finance. Far from the cold, rationalizing visions of Weber, Marx and Simmel, money plays a crucial role in qualitatively shaping social relations and in negotiating the boundaries between them.

Crowdfunding, then, is just one example of an attempt to humanize money, to reintroduce social values alongside technical descriptions of economic utility and value. And that mission – to reconnect value with values, and money with morality – is driving an 'ethical' revolution that is beginning to weaken the conventions of mainstream finance led by 'responsible investment' challenges from FinTech start-ups to challenger banks, from 'ethical' wealth managers to credit unions. As such, recognizing and better understanding the relationality of money is vital to this wider effort to democratize finance.

It's relational work, stupid!

When Isaac Newton was exploring the laws of motion and developing his theory of gravity, he observed closely the movement of objects in controlled conditions. His success in finding a grand theory, which for 300 years was used to predict the motions of everything from steam engines to planets, reflects an ambition that has never been fully lost by science despite the subsequent and wholesale replacement of Newton's theoretical basis by Albert Einstein.

Newton's problem was that his theory required a perspective that was abstract from the universe in question: the watchmaker. Orthodox theories of money demonstrate a similar approach, abstracting the calculation of value from the world and placing it into an equation. Money, reduced to its function as a medium for exchange, a measurement of value, and so on, is easy to see as flat and uniform, just as Simmel argued, as a technical object far removed from emotion and desire. In this understanding of money, social and cultural norms and values are simply an interference to the rational calculation of objective value. This philosophical standpoint is taken to extremes within the world of finance, reducing whole companies and markets to the shifting numbers of indices and portfolios that move independently of measuring any underlying 'purpose' or social value those companies may represent. It is important to recognize that the success of the FTSE4Good, an index of companies who conform to questionable standards of ESG (Environment, Social and Governance) has not yet led to the publication of its mirror index, a 'FTSE4Bad'.[14] Instead, the rises and falls of 'value' as calculated by the markets are reported as if they represent something meaningful to society, as opposed to monitoring which stocks are currently winning Keynes's 'beauty contest'.[15]

What more contemporary sociological and anthropological approaches to money reveal, however, is that this interference is not a function of irrational 'bias', but instead a vital part of what money is for in the first place. Money is not rational, but *relational*. Money is a social medium unlike any other in its chameleon ability to reflect the beliefs, values and norms of the cultures within which it operates – one of the reasons why anything can be 'money', as we learn from Mellor's work. The risk is that we have come to privilege forms of money and finance that conform to those four misconceptions of 'real money' and thus position anything else as somehow economically flawed.

The leading voice urging us to recognize this social meaning of money is Viviana A. Zelizer and, exchanging the dollar for sterling, we draw across her work in the US to consider a quick example.[16] Let's assume that you, dear reader, contact a significant other in your life – a partner, or a parent, perhaps – and inform them that you have 'spent' £2,000. How might they react? Now let's imagine that instead, you tell them you have managed to 'save' £2,000. Would that change their reaction? Saving money contributes precious little to society or the economy, as we saw in Chapter Three, acting as a form of value extraction that takes money out of circulation and away from making things happen. And yet, as authors we imagine your significant other(s) would be happier that you had saved rather than spent.

Let's now go one step further. What if you announced that you had 'invested' £2,000? What kind of a reaction might that cause? Would they hear 'invested' and conclude that you had 'gambled', 'lost' or 'thrown away' your £2,000? And yet, contrary to saving the money, a responsible investment in something that you believe in and that helps to build a society that reflects your wider moral view of the world – say a local community project or a renewable energy installation – is directly helping to drive the kinds of social changes you want to see happen in the world.

Sociologically speaking, the fact that we choose to see money only as a means of payment, as simply consumer spending power, rather than as something to be saved or invested in line with our values, opens up a space for thinking about what money *does* rather than what money *is* – a crucial first step in seeking to change the destination of money. Rather than asking 'what is money?', we urge people to ask, 'what does money do and could it do other, better things for society?'. People tend not to act from an understanding of what money is, but from a set of beliefs about money and its value that is predominantly social and cultural, rather than economic. This is why understanding the purpose of money is more meaningful than simply describing its function.

The idea that money is nothing more than consumer spending power also results in the mistaken positioning of 'the consumer as the principal lever of change'.[17] That we can, and should, shop our way to a better future. If you want to change the world, so this line of thinking goes, then you ought to buy this product and not that product. And if you are the kind of shopper who cares about equality, justice and the environment, the market is there to ensure that products exist wrapped in the promotional veneer of the more 'ethical' choice (for a premium price, obviously). But please, whatever you do, keep buying stuff at the same, or preferably a higher, rate as before. The consumer market can never offer the more 'ethical' choice, ostensibly accessible to far more people than those who can afford the premium, which is to choose to buy *less* stuff. If one fantasizes about having more money – and if we are honest with ourselves, who among us does not – then chances are the fantasy is intimately tied to a series of consumer purchases seen to mark important transitions across the life course. Seldom does the fantasy of having more money come with an image of the kinds of positive and purposeful investments one hopes to make.

Perhaps as a consequence, through current accounts, savings accounts, cash ISAs and pensions, instead people habitually hand over their 'unspent' money to a set of financial institutions that are openly cited as among the least trusted in society, precisely because *they* 'caused the crash', 'refused the loan', 'hiked interest rates on credit cards, again' (and yes, during an extended period of almost zero cost to them). According to the popular perception of how banks work, as outlined in Chapter Two, those same financial institutions then leverage and lend out these deposits to make investments in ways that, people are simply left to hope will somehow reflect their values. It's a rare thing when they do, and it requires considerable effort to demand transparency and to redirect investments backed by those deposits and thus in the name of people themselves.

To be clear, we do not mean to imply that shopping 'ethically' and following the path of the sustainable consumer is to be wholly avoided – far from it, assuming one can afford the premium to do so – but here's why analysing money in a sociological way is important. Being proud of a bamboo toothbrush as an ethical consumer choice is all well and good, but if sustainable products are being paid for by using a smartphone app provided by a series of companies that each refuse their tax obligations, or purchased via a debit or credit card offered by a major high-street bank that refuses to divest from carbon-intensive investments, then it just might be that this particular ethical consumer choice is in other ways also unwittingly contributing to a set of complex financial processes that are driving the very damaging outcomes to people and planet that choosing to 'shop ethically' is intended to avoid. Indeed, we provocatively suggest that the average consumer puts far more thought into the ethical credentials of which 'posh coffee' they buy each morning, than they do into which bank account or smartphone app they just tapped on the card machine in order to pay for it.

So, if money is more than consumer spending power, and needs to be used differently in order to deliver more positive outcomes, then how can we begin to understand it anew? One way is to recognize from our own experiences that we treat money very differently depending upon how it comes into our possession and from whom we have received it. Here we draw again on Zelizer's more sophisticated sociological explanation of these ideas, so let's consider another example of how money is *relational*, rather than rational.

Following Zelizer, we can say that – contrary to the mainstream economist's view that money is a set of neutral functions; and contrary to the classical 'Western' sociological view that money erodes bonds between people, converting them into relations between things – social relations not only survive but actively shape our understanding and use of money in ways that allow us to propose that no two £20 notes are necessarily the same. This stands in stark contrast to what the materiality of money as an object appears to tell us. Viewed in hand, two £20 notes certainly look and feel the same as each other. Each is inscribed with the same images and lettering. Each can be exchanged for goods and services that have been priced up to the amount of £20.

And yet, Zelizer teaches us that they are also very different. For example, a £20 note received as a gift from a much-loved grandparent is fundamentally different to a £20 note received as part of a monthly salary payment to which one is entitled. On the one hand, they may be 'worth' the same in terms of their functional economic value; but on the other, they are also 'worth' very different things socially because of the value placed upon the relationships that surround them. Simply put, money means different things to us because of its differing *relational* value. As Evans neatly summarizes:

> Zelizer's point is that fungibility of money is granted or suspended based on changes in social values and meaning, not based on market utility. A dollar of 'pin money' was not the same as a dollar of a husband's income, nor was a dollar of summer vacation money the same as a dollar of grocery money. A dollar of cash, while identical in quantity to a dollar's worth of food stamps, could not negotiate the social challenges of government aid to the poor, nor could it provide the same combination of social meaning and spending flexibility as a carefully chosen gift certificate. This vision of money provides a stark contrast to a theory of money based on market utility.[18]

This insight also has important consequences. How we choose to spend, save or invest any given £20 note is shaped significantly by the social relations that surround it, and therefore not only via a rational calculation of utility. And this is why choosing to spend, save or invest a £20 note, or the £2,000 lump sum we discussed earlier, is not governed by whether one or not the other option is more rational; but instead by money's role in what Zelizer calls 'relational work' and 'boundary marking'.[19] Spending on new clothes the £20 that your grandmother had given to you with a handwritten note hoping you might choose to save it for a rainy day may be considered morally hazardous, a slight on the relationship you enjoy with her, even if what you had bought could from another perspective be deemed to be rational.

One of the great lessons of Zelizer's relational approach to money is that it refutes Simmel's statement that money eradicates social bonds and reciprocity. In fact, we can see that the opposite is true. Money is a vital system of social trust that is essential for the creation, negotiation and maintenance of social bonds between people and, by establishing a shared agreement over its purpose, the destination of money can be to everyone's collective benefit.

Expanding this point, we can begin to open up other ways of seeing what money *does* – by marking out boundaries for the negotiation of multiple social relationships of different meaning – and see how, in countless areas of our lives, we decide to allocate (or using Zelizer's term, 'earmark') money to different purposes as shaped by meaningful social relations.[20] Since how we choose to spend, save, borrow and invest makes a material difference to the kind of world we are creating for ourselves and for future generations, it is vital to grasp how our understanding and use of money is already governed by social relationships that make particular monies more or less meaningful to us.

If, as Simmel argued, *money represents a claim upon society*, then we propose that through Zelizer's work we can begin to invert that principle in order to suggest instead that *society ought to be making claims upon money*, redirecting it in new and alternative ways that offer a better chance of positive social and environmental outcomes. By refusing to accept that money has a 'flat, colourless and heartless' nature, we start to recognize its other purpose as the most powerful tool for social change human societies have ever created, and so its capacity to respond to the triple threat of Climate, COVID-19 and Care. But it is going to require us to *do* different things with our money, and this is where crowdfunding steps in.

The gift of money

From the earliest explorations of modern anthropology, the question of money has been controversial. Bronislaw Malinowski, the founding father of social anthropology and modern ethnographic research, famously described the use of Kula shells as central to the economic and social life of a complex society built on very different principles of exchange to those which have become dominant in the West today.[21] In his seminal book *The Gift*, the financial journalist and anthropologist Marcel Mauss challenged the assumptions that gift exchange, and thus the principle of reciprocity as demonstrated within the Kula system, was not simply altruism standing in contrast to 'real' economic and financial negotiations of market exchange. Keith Hart describes the political and economic context for Mauss's radical rethinking of the basic assumption that capitalism, and the idea of the individual, somehow represent the natural human state.[22] To challenge that view, Hart produces an alternative archaeology of exchange that is built upon reciprocity and gifting, an archaeology that shows capitalism – at least what became the neoliberal version of it that has shaped its progress in the last 40 years – is simply an extreme version, rather than a long-standing foundation.

Money is not a technological gift to humankind, but was rather born from the needs of communities, whether scattered islands in the Pacific or the colonial empires of Europe, to exchange goods in the forms of gifts or trade, and to maintain and sustain both physical well-being and social relations. Similar patterns of exchange and gifting are to be found in the structure of the system of *eranos* loans in ancient Athens, discussed in Chapter Three, which played a role in many of the structures of crowdfunding and P2P finance that today make up alternative finance in the 21st century. As Hart states:

> There are two prerequisites for being human: we must each learn to be self-reliant to a high degree and to belong to others, merging our identities in a bewildering variety of social relationships. Much of modern ideology emphasizes how problematic it is to be both self-interested and mutual. Yet the two sides are often inseparable in practice and some societies, by encouraging private and public interests to coincide, have managed to integrate them more effectively than ours. Human institutions everywhere are founded on the unity of individual and society, freedom and obligation, self-interest and concern for others. The pure types of selfish and generous

economic action obscure the complex interplay between our individuality and belonging in subtle ways to others.[23]

This profoundly sociological insight explains why we find it difficult to explore new theories of money that may help to deliver more positive social, economic and environmental outcomes. And yet, to borrow from Franklin D. Roosevelt, we must 'above all, try something'. It is fortunate, then, that today we are blessed with some of the most ambitious heterodox economic ideas to help rethink our assumptions about money and finance.

Modern Monetary Theory, moonshots and missions to Mars

Stephanie Kelton's landmark contribution to finance's own Copernican Revolution comes by gazing through the lens of the planet-shifting possibilities of Modern Monetary Theory (MMT).[24] Like Mary Mellor, Kelton is keen to fight the deeply held conviction that government finances are just like household finances. Unlike households, governments can issue their own currency and so don't need first to 'find' the money before they can spend it. Unlike households, the government can never go broke in its own currency. 'Finding' the money to solve all of our major public problems – as if it required a grand quest of discovery, needing to be unearthed by life's most adventurous characters, as if it must surely come 'from somewhere' – isn't itself the problem. These myths about money have governed societies for nearly half a century. Convincing the public that Thatcher's 1983 speech, quoted earlier, and the neoliberal regime her grocer's worldview helped to build, was wrong about money is one of the biggest challenges facing those who wish to see a more democratic finance.

One of the starting points for MMT is that the relationship between democracy and finance is the wrong way around. Focusing primarily upon monetary sovereign nations that issue their own fiat currencies, Kelton argues that far from balancing the books, the role of the state is in fact to run a healthy deficit by investing in the things communities need to build a fairer and more sustainable world, using the sovereign currency to balance the expenditure. Two ideas follow from this that challenge conventional myths about money. First, damn it all, debt – if used in the right way – is good for societies. Second, the government does not have to turn to the taxpayer *before* it is able to spend into the economy. This is because, unlike the adventurer image of the 1848 Californian Gold Rush just alluded to, the government doesn't need to embark on a quest to 'find' new money in order to act. As the currency issuer, it is the government itself that finances government expenditure, not the taxpayer. Indeed, it is only the government that can (legally) issue that fiat currency. Kelton captures this idea in a neat pair of acronyms that reveal why it is important to grasp the destination of money and to understand in which direction it flows. Kelton's acronyms are (TAB)S – meaning tax and borrow before spending, representing the conventional view of the direction in which money flows, from the people to the state, as in Thatcher's representation – and S(TAB) – meaning spending before tax and borrowing, representing MMT's Copernican-like inversion.[25]

In Kelton's view, we can begin to see the logic in the S(TAB) framing when we recognize that we would have nothing with which to pay our taxes if the government – as the currency issuer – hadn't first already spent some money into existence. Furthermore, the coincidental timing of Kelton's book mean that these ideas have landed among the public in the middle of a live empirical test, as governments around the world respond to the COVID-19 pandemic by suddenly 'finding' money in order to fund various job retention programmes, such as the UK's 'furlough' scheme, apparently without the need first to raise taxes. And, as we know all too well, they also suddenly 'found' the money necessary to bail out the banks back in 2008 through the measures described as QE, a process that is still ongoing. The decade or more of austerity measures in between these two timely discoveries are thus revealed for what they always were – a *political* choice, not an economic one. Precisely because sovereign governments have the power to issue their own currencies, they can always do so for those occasions it deems necessary.

Kelton's analysis also means that the social and public policy implications of MMT become staggeringly clear, as the options on the table to address welfare provision, climate change, health and social care, homelessness and education no longer need to pass the test of financial feasibility in quite the same way. While real limits to what the government could and should do remain, in order to manage inflationary pressures, Kelton urges us to see the difference between the real limits of government expenditure and those myth-based limits that are political, and so a matter for democracies, not economic, and so a matter for 'independent' financial elites. Monetary sovereign countries do not need to 'find' the money to fund the things that their societies urgently need and to which, by virtue of their democratic citizenship, they ought to be entitled. In contrast to narratives of scarcity, MMT invites us to see the opportunities of fiscally responsible abundance.

Another enduring myth is that the private sector is the most capable of deciding upon the correct destination of money. This myth is of a dynamic, creative, colourful and entrepreneurial private sector that simply needs to be 'unleashed' from regulatory constraints. In turn, the state is depicted as necessary for fixing 'market failures' but otherwise as inherently bureaucratic, slow, grey and 'meddling' in economic matters.

Exploding this myth has been the principal target in a series of books by the economist Mariana Mazzucato. In *The Entrepreneurial State*, Mazzucato patiently documents through empirical examples how the vast majority of Promethean-like innovation is actually sparked by sustained investment in the public sector.[26] When the government decides that the best destination for public money is to spend it on research and development in universities, for example, it provides the 'patient capital' necessary to facilitate what Mazzucato calls 'mission-oriented investments' in the vital infrastructure that our communities require.

Mazzucato's concept of patient capital necessarily has the important consequence of positioning the capital of private finance as *impatient*, moving at such colossal speed and held in its most liquid form for as long as possible such that making direct investment in building tangible assets and infrastructure is almost impossible. The vast majority of financial structures intended to facilitate the investment of private capital are guided not by the anticipated social or environmental benefits of the physical asset or infrastructure being created in the real world, but instead by the rental incomes, interest rates and shareholder margins that can be achieved by provisioning impatient capital to such enterprises.[27] It is little wonder that Mazzucato continues to argue that we need a revolution in our theory of value.[28]

In her latest book, *Mission Economy*, Mazzucato draws inspiration from John F. Kennedy's 'moonshot' ambition, arguing that it is a useful frame for the type of civic collaboration needed to deliver better policy outcomes when confronting today's major social, environmental, health and economic challenges.[29] Civic collaboration means getting the private and public sectors truly to collaborate on building long-term, mission-oriented investment solutions that put people and planet before private profit. As with the massive mobilization of resources necessary for 1969's moon landing event, Mazzucato urges the public sector to be bold, showing leadership by driving forward the process of shared problem solving through coordinating cross-sector efforts in a 'symbiotic and mutualistic eco-system' with small, medium and large private companies.[30] National and local governments need to invest in their own internal capabilities and cease the practice of endlessly outsourcing tasks and processes to private firms and individuals, who likewise are impatient for financial rewards and are seldom fully invested in the long-term operational capacities of the public sector.

One way of doing this, Mazzucato suggests, is to change public sector tendering and procurement processes to shift from a principle of 'picking winners' to one of 'picking the *willing*' – that is, to privilege those who demonstrate the greater willingness to collaborate on delivering shared and mutually beneficial outcomes.[31] And Mazzucato is clear, this really is about market-making and risk-taking by the public sector, just as much as it is about market-fixing and de-risking. What is desperately needed to facilitate this effort is a renewed sense of *purpose*, something we have been arguing for throughout this book. Only by reconnecting our money and our democracy with an outcome-focused, mission-oriented sense of purpose can we hope to rekindle a clear sense of what our money and our democracy is *for*.

Taking the 'moonshot' idea very literally, though aiming at a different destination with his money, Elon Musk – the global entrepreneur and founder of the electric vehicle company Tesla Inc. – is reportedly developing a vehicle capable of extended space travel. *Starship*, to grant the vehicle its full and less than imaginative title, is described as a fully reusable transport system capable of carrying up to one hundred people to Mars. The founding ethos of Musk's privately-owned spaceflight company, *SpaceX*, is to 'make life multi-planetary'.[32] Motivated in part by the perceived existential threats of a forthcoming asteroid collision capable of wiping out humanity, Musk believes that the very survival of *homo sapiens* as a species depends upon becoming a spacefaring civilization. In 2016, while outlining his project at an international conference in Mexico, Musk stated "I hope you would agree [this] is the right way to go."[33]

As fellow billionaires Jeff Bezos and Richard Branson also begin to get lost in space, there are presumably plenty of people willing to tell Musk boldly where to go. For us, the *SpaceX* mission to Mars is instructive in at least two ways. First, there is an apparent acquiescence to the idea that humanity is on course for a social and environmental collapse that cannot now be averted. The only option for the species (and it's hard to write this with any degree of seriousness) is to leave the planet. As we have insisted upon throughout this book, there truly is a clear and present danger to the future of human civilizations and countless species happening right now here on Earth. If not averted in time, the catastrophic effects of climate breakdown really will, within a matter of decades, end life as we have known it for millennia. But Musk appears to have fallen hard for the variously attributed injunction that it is easier to imagine the end of the world than it is to imagine even the smallest change to the way capitalism operates.[34] For us, there remains time and ideas yet to resist the escapist urge and instead work towards that smallest change. Secondly, the mission to Mars is a good example of staring at a 'moonshot' ambition through the wrong end of a telescope. Whereas Mazzucato's ambition is to repurpose our economies and our politics in pursuit of the public good, Musk's vision for a spacefaring civilization is driven largely by elite private capital and a personal sense of adventure.

It is not for us to say whether or not blasting billionaires into orbit may ultimately contribute to humanity's survival. Perhaps it's worth a try. But we remain convinced that, for some time yet, trying to solve our earthly problems still deserves to be the destination of money. Fixing a financial system than has enabled a few individuals to amass enough wealth to embark upon the same space travelling ambitions that once required entire nation states to accomplish seems like a good place to start. What we learn from both Kelton and Mazzucato is that the question to be asked is not, as Musk may wish, '*how much money is there and what can I do with it?*' Instead, inspired by their work, the question becomes '*what needs doing and how do we change the destination of money to deliver those outcomes?*' At different stages of this book, we have demonstrated that there is already plenty of money in circulation. MMT is the latest iteration in a long-standing and evidence-based argument that governments with fiat currencies are never short of money because they can create more of it by spending into the economy.

What is desperately needed to meet the social and environmental challenges of now, therefore, is a colossal spending programme to meet the needs of everyone in our communities. The framework of a Green New Deal, which could provide such a programme, has to date been a missed opportunity. The decision of our governments not to spend is a *political* and not an economic choice. Given that what is so urgently needed are new financial channels, as part of a collective effort to redirect money with a clear sense of purpose towards delivering better outcomes for people and planet, we propose that crowdfunding and P2P finance represent one of the best options for engaging citizens in building a mission economy together.

As Marie Ekeland so eloquently put it, to invest is to shape the future. All money needs is a destination. The question before us is simple: do you only want to follow the wind, or would you rather make it blow?

FIVE

Futures of Democratic Finance

In exploring new ways of seeing money and finance, this book has aimed to empower and embolden the reader to start to look at money differently and to question the purpose of our finance system, both what it is now and what it should be. After all, alternative finance was created by a wide social movement across business, academia and civil society, involving many collaborations between people outside of finance with those who were and are utterly disaffected within it.

As well as encouraging more social movements to see the importance of money and finance for furthering their own causes, we hope also that many more practitioners within the finance industry will begin to challenge themselves to develop financial innovations that are founded upon a belief that money can be a force for public good and that finance ought to be more than a complex machine for creating and extracting private profit. The world out there is not an external resource to be mined in the interests of creating financial value. That world out there is nothing less than the lives of billions of people and countless other species in the natural world. The future of finance needs to take far greater care of both if it is to keep hold of its social licence and play a role in delivering the transformation we need to protect people and planet from the urgent threats that both currently face.

In this final chapter, we extend our analysis to set out what we think are some of the most pressing and difficult questions that need to be addressed if we are to free our understanding of finance from its gilded cage and continue our journey towards a world were money is something social, collaborative, account-able, democratic and sustainable. Right now, however, there are those who would interpret the mission of democratizing finance in a very different way to us, seeking to remove the state completely and further eradicate human decision-making from the apparently smooth functioning of tech-enhanced market mechanisms. The rise of distributed ledger technolo-gies (DLTs) such as blockchain, and the cryptocurrencies and cryptoassets these technologies have created, has been interpreted by many as a democratic revolution — putting power into the code-writing hands of people who are free to manage transactions without the need for such cumbersome legacy hardware as banks, law firms and governments. In what follows, we outline the dangers we see in this particular version of democratic finance, along with some wider thoughts on the taboos over investment, how to nurture magic money trees and why it's important to be able to recognize wealth creation from wealth management.

While each sub-section can be read in sequence, they can also be read in isolation, offered as a series of provocations on the futures of democratic finance in the hope of inspiring others to contribute to these debates. To begin, let us consider those current trends that we can already see shaping the future of our primary focus throughout this book, namely crowdfunding and P2P finance.

Challenging crowdfunding, within and without

What should be clear by now is that crowdfunding and P2P finance are a diverse global phenomenon that reach far beyond the definition we had at the start of the book about a quick and simple way to donate small sums of money to charitable and other 'goodwill' causes. The valuable work by CCAF, co-founded by the visionary scholar Bryan Zhang (someone else who likes to ask, 'what is money doing?'), has charted through a series of quantitative survey reports the rise of more than 1,800 platforms worldwide. This work, discussed in Chapter Two, is invaluable for getting a grasp of the size and volume of crowdfunding and P2P markets around the world. In adopting a mainly quantitative approach, however, there is some distance still to travel fully to understand how different social and cultural contexts are helping to shape the development of crowdfunding in any given nation or across a particular region. As a result, perhaps we should not expect the future of crowdfunding to be dictated by those global financial centres such as London, Berlin, Shanghai or San Francisco that so proudly house the world's sector-leading 'FinTech hubs'. Instead, the revolution in thought and practice that we outlined in Chapter One is more likely to come from new areas of innovation, as countries and regions in East Asia, Latin America and other parts of the Global South seek to develop financial systems that learn from and so are able to avoid those legacy problems and perpetual crises that have beset the 'Washington consensus' model.[1] For example, during the early stages of the crowdfunding and P2P finance industry, the UKCFA was contacted by ministers from the Argentinian government who wanted to understand whether P2P finance offered an alternative to a system of business finance that was dominated by (regularly failing) banks. The experience of countries adopting these models is that they have watched, learned and innovated from the experiences in the West.

The UK's crowdfunding and P2P sectors, which until recently were viewed as a world leader in terms of both regulation and innovation, have come under sustained pressure from the FCA who have themselves come under significant pressure and political criticism for their handling and policing of unregulated (and allegedly fraudulent) investments, which in a desperate grab for legitimacy and credibility hitched themselves via 'boiler-room' style marketing practices onto the alternative finance sector's solid reputation. The consequences of these malpractices by unscrupulous entrants to the alternative finance space was that many customers were left holding inappropriate investments, or losing their money altogether, without any recourse to complaint or to compensation afforded to regulated investment companies.

Dame Gloster's official review of these unhappy episodes, discussed in Chapter Two, pointed to stark failings in the ability of the regulator's monitoring and even understanding of the alternative finance market.[2] In the short term, this has led to the creation of new rules that have put real constraints on the growth and future innovation of the crowdfunding and P2P sectors. Hopefully, valuable lessons are now being learned and better systems of monitoring and enforcement are in place, so there will be a return to much needed competition in order more positively to disrupt the mainstream finance market in the UK and beyond. Exciting new propositions, such as the next generation of platforms now emerging, will be borne of very different understandings of money and finance that exist around the world, especially in the Global South.[3]

That being said, the development of new forms of 'civic' finance in the UK – such as the CMI structure that we helped to create – are beginning to provide a potential antidote to other failed models, such as Private Finance Initiative (PFI) and Public-Private Partnership (PPP) schemes. These more corporate-facing models of investment sought to use private capital to build public projects, resulting in what are considered to be very generous rewards for the apparent risks and costs of failure, but that were typically socialized and underwritten by the public sector. By harnessing investment direct from the public through crowdfunding models, like CMIs, levels of transparency and citizen engagement are created that can help to (re) build trust based on a sharing of social responsibilities, rather than relying upon ever more complex legal contracts where the counterparty with the most expensive lawyers invariably wins.

The biggest change affecting the whole financial system from top to bottom, however, is the growth and growing scrutiny of ESG investing. The driver here is a huge shift in generational attitudes regarding the urgency of action needed on the Climate Emergency, combining a growing unease over the practices of mainstream finance with a rising awareness that private companies only account for social and environmental costs as externalities to be held 'off balance sheet'. This trend no doubt will be accelerated further by the biggest intergenerational transfer of wealth, set to occur in the next 10–20 years, as tens of trillions are inherited from the so-called post-war 'Boomer' generation by their increasingly 'Doomer' children and 'Zoomer' grandchildren, that is the financially marginalized members of 'Generation X' and the 'Millennials'. What is already clear is that these new generations of investors have very different values and goals for their money, which is accelerating the pressure on mainstream financial institutions to shift from 'neutral' to 'drive' when it comes to action on addressing the Climate Emergency and those equally pressing issues such as social care, access to fair and secure housing and intensifying intersectional inequalities in all our communities.

The structural nature of this shift was underlined by an announcement in the March 2021 Budget Speech, made by the current UK Chancellor Rishi Sunak, that the Bank of England's Monetary Policy Committee and the Bank's market operations (that is, those who buy investments in the market) should do so with the objective 'to reflect the government's economic strategy for achieving strong, sustainable and balanced growth that is also environmentally sustainable and consistent with the transition to a net zero economy'.[4] This represents the biggest change in UK monetary and finance policy since the independence of the Bank of England itself was announced on 6 May 1997.[5]

The democratic principles that underpinned the development of the crowdfunding and P2P finance sectors now appear to be influencing the financial Leviathan, which is rapidly seeking to ensure they are not disadvantaged in terms of their medium-term financial return. As such, new smartphone app-based forms of investment – ranging from the headline-grabbing day traders on Robin Hood to emerging forms of 'ethical investment' services, such as Tickr and Big Exchange – are placing positive social and environmental impact on justice and sustainability at the top of the list of priorities for their customers.[6] This is fuelling a rise in what is being called 'activist stewardship', where so-called 'universal holders' – a phrase coined by Ellen Quigley – are unable simply to divest themselves of certain 'bad' stocks, but instead use their significant market power to change company strategies to steer a course towards a net zero world.[7] In this respect, we are seeing the development of forms of representative democracy operating in the conventional finance world, alongside the cut and thrust of direct action and more deliberative approaches in crowdfunding.

Understanding investment as a social act

We've had several occasions already to engage with Mark Carney's 2020 Reith lectures, delivered at a key writing phase of this book, during which Adam Smith's famous book *The Wealth of Nations* was discussed. Smith's metaphor of the 'invisible hand' is today evoked as if it were a natural law, offered as a way to justify a multitude of financial sins. We, however, are particularly interested in how the idea has been used to suggest that financial markets should focus on their 'knitting', namely increasing private wealth, and leave the public good to politicians. In other words, finance ought to put profit before people and planet in all of its activities, because anything else should be the task of government.

We agree with Carney that anyone actually reading Smith's book would do well also to read its predecessor, *The Theory of Moral Sentiments*. Those who do so will quickly realize that the metaphor for the social benefits of self-interest, which Smith creates in those few very brief passages of *The Wealth of Nations* that deal with the 'invisible hand', at best paint only half the picture of what Smith imagined was needed to create a truly 'wealthy nation'. Smith, somewhat naively it seems, assumed that anyone interested in reading *The Wealth of Nations* would be doing so having already absorbed the important lessons contained within its predecessor, *The Theory of Moral Sentiments*, lest those brief passages on the 'invisible hand' be later taken out of context, misunderstood, and mistakenly used to govern an extractive financial system for half a century or more.

Smith argues that prudence, understood as 'thriftiness' or a 'savings culture', is vital for survival. This is a philosophy that we now know resonates as much with Xenophon's Socrates as it does with Margaret Thatcher's father, yet Smith insists it is not sufficient for a society to thrive. Domestic platitudes such as 'look after the pennies and the pounds will look after themselves' reflect the values of prudence and thrift in a household (*oikos*) with a clear boundary established to a world of money 'outside' of the home, something we learned from Zelizer. For Smith, however, this philosophy should not detract from encouraging the social side of ourselves that tends towards altruism and generosity to others, what he called 'beneficence'. This desire to create positive good for others, in Smith's estimation, should remain a question of choice rather than rules, but nevertheless the society that encourages its citizens to think beyond prudence and justice and to consider 'beneficence' is far better off and happier than one that believes money should be a wholly private affair, directed only at personal enrichment.

In many ways, the principles of crowdfunding and P2P finance are built on this more optimistic view of an individual's social nature, as they seek to align money more transparently with moral sentiments than to cede power to any form of invisible hand offered by mainstream finance. After all, money is far more likely to be put towards ventures that contribute to the public good if the decision over its allocation is one that takes place in a social rather than an individual setting. Morality is not something to be calculated and weighed up, as a consumer might do in front of a shelf of products. Instead, morality is something that confronts us when we are face-to-face with others in society. In such proximate circumstances, we not only feel responsibility for the others' needs, but we can also acquire a better sense of others' altruistic motivations to help others, which then further inspires us to try to solve problems that are not ours alone to solve.

In other words, there are no biographical solutions to systemic problems, as both Ulrich Beck and Zygmunt Bauman were fond of saying, but countless examples of collective efforts to help each other in periodic states of emergency show that we are capable and willing to come together to assist each other in ways that are only made possible by the spontaneous gathering of a crowd.[8] This is one reason why we have seen far earlier adoption of ESG investing among the wider crowdfunding fraternity than elsewhere in the financial system. It perhaps also explains why it was the online social forums of Reddit, rather than the frictionless trading systems of the share platforms, which encouraged individual investors to put their money at risk in the GameStop episode in order to fight what they saw as the injustice of the aggressive short trader on the Wall Street markets.[9]

In contrast, as we will return to at the end of this chapter, the ethos of the Bitcoin community is one that celebrates the individual in apparently splendid isolation. Although Bitcoin provides an alternative to the hierarchical systems of trust in mainstream finance, somewhat literally embodied in their skyscrapers and marble pediments, the effect of its technologically enabled 'distributive' model of trust is the further individualization and privatization of money. The instinct is somewhat analogous to today's 'prepper' and survivalist communities, or the early eco-activists who use their capital to invest in systems of provision while also going 'off grid', a decision that if it were to be taken collectively would only be counterproductive to the achievement of the collective objective of a net zero society.

The limits of extreme self-interest and leaving things to the 'invisible hand' are here laid bare. All too often, the regulators of finance start from the assumption that the investor is *Homo economicus*, Pierre Bourdieu's 'anthropological monster', an apparently self-interested and instrumentally rational individual concerned only with calculating optimal gains from their activities.[10] As a consequence of this ontological image, regulators rely far too heavily on rules and incentives rather than taking the time to understand the benefits of seeing the investor more holistically as also a person with a family whom they wish to provide for, perhaps with grandchildren whose future they wish to protect, and with a vast swathe of other anxieties and dreams that lend them to being more interdependent and social beings than the cold, calculating 'monster' they are assumed to be. Seen in the context of their social relations to others, it becomes possible for finance to function while also delivering more purposeful outcomes for society as a whole.

The all too narrow focus upon what constitutes an investor, however, results in a lowest common denominator system that, in Smith's terms, unduly privileges prudence at the expense of moral sentiments. The depersonalization of the investment decision, whether through traders sitting alone at their Bloomberg terminals or the still more non-human process of automated algorithmic trading, is causing an alternative 'tragedy of the horizon' by creating a system built on an ideal of prudent self-interest that fails to produce a thriving society. The challenge is to explode finance out of being an exclusive club, as the City of London became in the 20th century, when membership of the right golf club was a better predictor of securing venture finance for your latest business idea than the quality of outcomes sought by the idea itself.

This is precisely the challenge that crowdfunding and P2P finance have taken seriously, not only by refusing to start from the assumptions about *Homo economicus*, but also by encouraging a far more diverse community of people to see themselves as investors capable of making real change in the world. Indeed, the founders of crowdfunding platforms are far more representative of society than across the finance industry as a whole, where urgent change is also needed if we are genuinely to tackle the gendered regime in finance.[11]

The enduring paradox of financial inclusion

The invention of crowdfunding and P2P finance raises the issue of financial inclusion when it comes to investment, which – as we saw at the end of Chapter Two – is often framed alongside questions of how to improve access to banking for the 'unbanked' as well as access to credit. Are there some who shouldn't be permitted to use banks and to access credit? If not, then does including those currently excluded contribute to their further exploitation? Since the mainstream financial system is motivated by extracting value from clients, rather than serving the needs of society's most vulnerable citizens, ought we to focus upon the 'positive' side of being excluded from mainstream finance? If so, why should the majority of people already financially included continue to stay as such? And so it goes round.

The common assumption inside mainstream finance is that those who are marginalized and excluded on the basis of single characteristic or intersectional identities of age, economic status, ethnicity or gender somehow need to be educated in order to qualify to join the franchise of the 'banked', the 'invested' or the (note the normative inflection) 'creditworthy'. This makes the task of pursuing financial inclusion sound as worthy and necessary as maintaining and extending the democratic franchise within a nation state, or ensuring sufficient literacy and numeracy skills to operate in the market.

What we hope is clear from our analysis of the development of crowdfunding and P2P throughout this book is that we do not see the 'democratization' of finance, and particularly of investment, as somehow magically addressing the real and structural problems of injustice and inequity experienced by excluded groups interacting with the current finance system.

For all the opportunities we see in it, crowdfunding is not a panacea. What we do stress, however, is that the ideas that underpin crowdfunding and P2P finance are potentially beneficial to marginalized groups who are 'able to pay', in particular the principles of transparency, equality of access and placing people at the heart of decision-making processes. As we saw in Chapter Four, without the inclusion of a greater diversity of people in finance, it will continue to reflect the values and worldviews of a narrow group of older, male, White and relatively wealthy individuals.

The assumption that financial education is a main barrier to inclusion also needs to be called into question, since it locates the problem at the site of the individual, rather than with society as a whole. If within a society, only one individual is 'unbanked', then we may reasonably assume that this is because of something within that individual's character, their skills or immediate capabilities. In other words, perhaps it is that individual's private trouble and so it is better that an individual, biographical solution is pursued. But if within a whole society millions of people are 'unbanked', then we may reasonably assume that this is because of something within that society's character, reflecting the willingness and capabilities of that society to provide accessible and secure finance for everyone. In other words, in such an instance the social structure of finance has evidently collapsed leading to a major public issue, rather than an individual private trouble. As the progressive campaigns for an alternative form of finance have consistently argued, the causes of financial exclusion are social and thus require systemic change, instead of continuing to blame millions of individuals for their perceived lack of financial education.

Our experience of working inside and researching from outside the financial industry over the last two decades suggests that the belief in education as the primary solution is perhaps one of the most pernicious and iniquitous. The alternative perspectives on money and finance that we have highlighted here, across both sociology and anthropology, clearly demonstrate that excluded groups are far from 'living without money', as became a trend for certain activists to attempt in the years following the global crash in 2008. Instead, different groups adhere to different cultures of money, which is understood differently because of the values, beliefs and moralities through which money and finance operate. This is as true of the use of Kula shells in the Trobriand Islands as it is of Islamic Finance practices today. It isn't necessary to travel as far as Malinowski did to find competing understandings of money. They exist in the homes and minds of people all over the world, including here in the UK as one of the most financialized societies on the planet.

The insights of Zelizer, Falk and Maenpaa, and others show that financial vulnerability is not only a question of social characteristics or identity but also a function of one-off events, ranging from divorce and redundancy through to huge financial windfalls from inheritance or even gambling.[12] The effect is to create real stress and anxiety for the individual or household, distorting their decisions with the money received, which purely from a financial perspective seem irrational and at an individual level 'out of character' compared to their ability to make other forms of complex decisions in their lives.

Looking ahead, the enduring paradox of financial inclusion is a genuine test case for crowdfunding and P2P finance. Clearly, encouraging the inclusion and so deeper entanglement of vulnerable people in an exploitative mainstream financial system raises serious concerns. How far crowdfunding and P2P can demonstrate their alternative credentials to such a system will go a long way to attracting more than the usual suspects of White, male and retired investors to their cause. After all, if women are 'cautiously right' in their assessment of risk compared to 'confidently wrong' men, surely we should be encouraging women to make more investment decisions? A major problem, highlighted throughout the book, is that regulators continue to hold steadfast to their view that the 'ideal type' investor is a man taking rational decisions over how best to optimize his returns, rather than appreciating the complex social relations that surround investment decisions and how investors needn't only be older, White men.

What is clear is that crowdfunding and P2P finance represent a major challenge to the idea that the best way to organize our interactions around money and finance is to keep faith with the demonstrably false notion of a rational individual actor guided solely by the principles and calculations of self-interest when allowed to operate freely within markets. Their major challenge is based upon seeing the value of encouraging a more diverse group of people to get involved as investors, bringing a more reciprocal, social and democratic understanding of money that shifts the focus of financial innovation away from questions of the technical functionality of markets and instead towards its wider purpose in creating value for everyone in society.

The taboo of investment

In 1922, almost exactly 100 years ago at the time of writing, Malinowski published *Argonauts of the Western Pacific*, a revolutionary work that brought vividly to life the daily lives of Pacific Islanders at the turn of the 20th century. Malinowski was the first to exhort anthropologists to venture beyond the verandas and compounds of the British colonial infrastructure and instead attempt to learn from more direct, first-hand experience of the lives of the people beyond the picket fences.

Central to his depiction of Pacific Island life was the circulation of Kula shells, which were a form of currency for the islanders, a study that has been subsequently influential in the anthropological and sociological study of money. If Malinowski opened the door to new perceptions of society, it was his contemporary, Marcel Mauss, writing soon after in 1925, who first challenged Malinowski's assumptions about the value of gifts and gifting. Mauss saw in Malinowski's description a challenge to the idea that our 'Western' system of value, money and market exchange was in any sense a universal truth. Instead, he understood the nature of the exchange to be based on social rather than individual calculations of value.

Others, including the anthropologist Annette Weiner, later revisited the research site of Malinowski to discover his blind spot when it came to women in the exchange economy, especially the matrilineal nature of inheritance which shed new light on Mauss's initial insight into the nature of obligation and reciprocity in the idea of the gift.[13] Gifts, of course, represent an obligation and relationship which is relegated to a 'non-economic' altruistic plane in the conventions of modern market capitalism. But what if we regarded our own social life of money today with the same anthropological strangeness that Malinowski approached the Trobriand islanders? What if they were to turn their ethnographic gaze on modern 'Western' culture? They would find a society with its own curiosities and taboos when it comes to money and investment.

As we have seen from both the historical and contemporary examples provided throughout this book, the taboos which led Malinowski to emphasize the 'reciprocity' of gift exchange in contrast to a 'true gift' where no return favour is expected or given, are deeply rooted in the myths and stories which underpin our own beliefs in the value of money, the financial institutions which create and control it, and the role of investment in our daily lives. Understanding these taboos is vital to overcoming the barriers to democratization of investment in capitalist market economies. The age-old tensions between the private and public, domestic and commercial, rural and metropolitan, which we have seen in the accounts of finance and investment in ancient Athens from Hesiod, Plato, Xenophon and Aristophanes, are still writ large in our own beliefs and taboos about money.

The social life of money as experienced by people living in the 21st-century UK, for example, is very different to that experienced within the rarefied atmosphere of a bank or investment company. Despite our pretensions of 'progress', our use of money and finance is still very much 'embedded' in systems of kinship, religion and politics. Money and investments are not simply tools or technology to achieve an end. They have value in themselves based on what Arjun Appadurai called 'the social life of things'.[14] All manner of financial objects were found to be carrying meanings which reached far beyond simple measures of financial or even economic value. As we saw in Chapter Four, Zelizer and others within 'relational' economic sociology have shown that money is not neutral, and that how it comes into one's possession (be it earned, entitled, won, inherited or simply found) has a direct impact on whether we then decide to spend, save or invest it, and how. For the democratization of finance, and the growth of democratic forms of lending and investment, the most important boundaries to consider are between public and private, and between the domestic and the market (perhaps better expressed as between the *oikonomic* and the *economic*).

The first insight is that the embedded forms of exchange identified in what Karl Polanyi might term 'pre-capitalist' cultures are still very much in evidence within so-called 'developed' capitalist market economies.[15] Similar to Malinowski in the Pacific, we view these activities as somehow strange or marginal, but in reality they are highly influential in financial decision-making. What behavioural economists see as 'bias' is instead the manifestation of alternative belief systems which are oftentimes in direct conflict with the rules and practices of financial markets. Just one example is in setting levels of 'interest' on the Zopa platform and consideration of wider signifiers of trust beyond statistical correlation with financial behaviours.

The second insight centres on the role and meaning of money in the 'domestic' (*oikonomic*) sphere, in which, just as in the Trobriand Islands, the traditional role of women as the decision-maker and conserver of wealth and security is significantly ignored and underestimated by those within the finance industry. The dominant mode of accumulation of wealth is thus through saving and thrift, which is contrasted with the risk and potential for loss of the world of investment that is seen as drawing money away from the home and reducing security. This means that customers find the symbolism of finance undermines their confidence at the point of financial decision, such as a bank. Experimentation with removing the conventional symbolic capital of a bank and replacing them with signifiers of the domestic sphere made people more trusting of the institution.

The third insight relates to a politics of scarcity. Making money a scarce resource gives power to the holders of what in the financial world are called 'real assets'. The problem is that the biggest sceptics about the 'magic money tree' are those who would benefit the most, namely the holders of debt and the earners of wages. At another level, democratization is not just of ownership but also of creditor power over companies and governments.

The development of crowdfunding and P2P finance, and the challenges it has faced along the way from a sceptical political and regulatory establishment, has shown that it is possible to break some of these taboos and so create financial channels that are not only complementary to the rules of traditional financial markets, but also create social value and purpose above and beyond a narrow assessment of their economic function.

Money, meaning and those magic money trees

The English language is not short of words for running out of money. You can be skint, broke, brassic, flat, penniless, bankrupt, short, feeling the pinch or on your uppers. As the world's politicians emerged from the Excel Centre in London's Docklands more than a decade ago, declaring to have 'saved the world' by transferring huge amounts of money via QE to a banking system on the verge of collapse, the world was immediately informed that the bailout was not going to come for free. Regardless of its colossal size, the bailout was going to require extreme cuts to public services and a policy framework of austerity was pursued in order to 'balance the books'.

In 2021, trillions of dollars and pounds sterling have been mobilized to fight the COVID-19 pandemic and to keep society moving while large sections of the economy have been temporarily shut down. As the end of the pandemic slowly looms into view, the bills have apparently started to come in and already the same narrative is being reprised. We are going to have to pay back all the debt we've accrued through public spending, or else risk financial Armageddon. As the Overton window creaks open, once again inviting us to gaze out over the horizon at yet another decade of austerity, let's be clear that the money used to fund job retention schemes, to keep businesses solvent and to support public services has not been paid for with the state's credit card. As we have seen several times already, most notably in Chapter Four, the government's finances are not like a household's finances. These emergency measures in response to the crisis have in fact been paid for (hold on to your socks!) with *real money*.

We also saw in Chapter Four how misconceptions about 'real money' lead people into thinking some sorcery or conspiracy must be afoot when such claims are made, so let's be clear. Money is created by a sovereign government when it sells bonds, essentially a form of financial IOU, to its central bank, perhaps the Bank of England or the US Federal Reserve. There is therefore nothing to pay back, because the money wasn't borrowed from anyone else. It was created. Although the BBC News Channel in the UK broadcast this fact on 9 March 2021, stating quite clearly that 92 per cent of the money the UK government had spent on its emergency COVID-19 measures was created this way, popular myths about over-borrowing and debt mountains endure.[16] Ask most people on the street what they think about the way government creates money and it's likely one or all of the misconceptions about 'real money' will be rehearsed. The problem is not one of accounting. It is a problem of beliefs about money. As demonstrated back in Chapter One, it would appear that austerity measures have been rather good for the financial situation of billionaires and asset managers. The value of assets, property, shares and bonds have all risen. For those without those types of investments, which is the majority of people even in 'wealthy' countries such as the UK or the USA, well, there still isn't enough money to go around.

The British comedian Miles Jupp is fond of riffing on the subject of his privileged middle class stage persona. In one anecdote, he recalls a 'personal experience' of a street altercation with a young man in Hull, a port city on the East Coast of England. After an initial clash of accents, and an invitation for the young man to solve their miscommunication by enunciating properly using the diaphragm, the penny suddenly drops. Jupp realizes that he is about to be the victim of some "street aggression" when the young man shouts, "give me your money!". Jupp's reply to his assailant is instructive: "What all of it? Most of it's tied up in land. The paperwork's going to be an absolute nightmare."[17]

The joke hinges on two worlds of money: one where money is linked to assets, and one where cash comes and goes. Neither protagonist in the joke accurately describes what money is. The purpose of 'creating' money, as we have seen throughout the book, is not to create wealth and then give it to someone – as Jupp claims he ended up doing by writing the young man a cheque – but rather it is done to maintain trust in the idea of money itself.

Because it truly only exists as a belief system in our imagination, which accounts for the rich cultural life of money and finance throughout history and across the world today, then without trust in money, money ceases to exist. The problem of 'creating' money is that a careful balance needs to be struck between keeping money flowing and people trusting less in the value of money, such that they begin to question what they are prepared to do to acquire more of it. This is one of the reasons why central banks use an increasingly technical lexicon for what they call 'market operations', such as QE. So what is the problem with our belief about money? Why is it so far from the reality of money in society? And why is it ultimately unhelpful to talk about 'magic money trees'?

When people talk about 'real money', as Viviana A. Zelizer found when examining the concept of 'earmarking', people are typically talking either about money 'created' by work or money that itself has intrinsic value by being linked to a precious metal, such as gold. Bitcoin, which some have touted as the future of money and another way to democratize finance, has managed to merge both of these beliefs into its founding myth. The value of Bitcoin is both a function of 'proof of work' and 'the immutable line of computer code'. As such, Bitcoin's claim to be 'money' – as opposed to a simple invest-ment asset like a tulip bulb or a share certificate – is perhaps not as visionary as its advocates may wish us to believe. In its basic idea, Bitcoin takes us decidedly back to the future.

Taking the first of these, if we believe that we create money when we work (or put/waste energy into the 'system') then we discount uses of money which are not considered work in our economic system. We don't often ask ourselves why some forms of work 'create' more money than others. Those at the top of companies justify this by saying they 'create work' and therefore 'create wealth' for others (and reward themselves for it, just like Bitcoin miners with their energy hungry server farms). Where this myth starts to unravel is when you con-sider the fact that the money you are exchanging for your 'work' has no material value hidden somewhere in a vault. Its value is a function of the trust that people place in money to be accepted in return for something in the future by another human being. This means that if there is a shortage of money in the world, then it doesn't matter how valuable the work is that you do, or how valuable the object you want to sell, there won't be any money to pay for it.

In a similar way, when central banks or governments print money, they are not bringing any more 'value' into the world, but simply trying to keep people using money, which if people value it less (for example, if there is a loss of confidence in the currency) we need more of it to buy the things we need. So to say 'there *is* a magic money tree' is neither correct nor incorrect, but ultimately counterproductive to the argument against the assertion that 'there *isn't* enough money to go around'. We can make as much money as we want (there really is a magic tree), and making more money allows the finance and economic systems to function. But if people believe that making that extra money leads to a devaluing of the buying power of that money then they will want more of it when they work or sell things to get money to trade for other things they need.

We look next at what this means for the way in which we think about investment as a way to 'earn' money.

From wealth creation to wealth management: neoliberalism's 'real' legacy

What would the founding fathers of neoliberal thought really think about the situation we find ourselves in today? The massive concentration of wealth and the growth of inheritance to preserve both power and social position were exactly the things which Adam Smith saw being disrupted by the indus-trial revolution and the growth of private capitalism. Smith would have recognized the symptoms and problems of this concentration of wealth, but would he have recognized the role of finance in its realization?

We have explored two themes in this book, the impact of crowdfunding on the democratization of finance and the role and value of forms of crowdfunding to maximize the benefits of investment for the real economy and society. The need for financial innovation that promotes such outcomes becomes all too clear when you look behind the glass windows and image advertising of major financial institutions and actually examine what makes them tick (that is, how they make money themselves).

To the outsider, the financial centres of the City of London or New York are about sharp suits, tall buildings, taking risks and, of course, 'making money'. Since Dick Whittington 'turned again' the streets of the City have been paved with gold. But when you step inside the Square Mile, or walk along Wall Street, you find a very different idea of what 'makes money'. You will be struck by just how much of our financial system, its regulation, institutions, advisers and markets are in fact not focused on the creation of new wealth or activity in the real economy, but *the preservation of existing wealth.*

The reason for this is the simple economics of many financial institutions, economics that challenge crowdfunding platforms as much as they challenge the big investment houses. It is easier and more profitable to make money preserving wealth if you are a financial professional than the risky and difficult world of creating wealth from the real economy. The wealthier your client, the more valuable that service is to them and the more financial firepower you are able to acquire. There is a certain base cost of acquiring a customer and managing them which is the same if they invest £5 as if they invest £5,000 (in part this is a cost of regulation, but it is also the fact that all customers should be treated equally and fairly). As a result, companies are forced to balance the recruitment of lower value customers (upon some of whom they lose money servicing) with higher value investors who provide the lion's share of the company's profits. Some companies are willing to pay that price, to keep their services accessible, but the fact of the matter is that in a world brought up on the idea of 'free banking' (remember: if a service is free, you are the product) we are reluctant to pay for financial services unlike other forms of advice or support. On top of this, the growth of 'tax efficient' investment, offshore accounting and the global movement of capital has facilitated a simultaneous shift in the priorities of the finance system, away from its value to society and towards its ability to extract profit from the activities of investment and finance. If you follow the money, you will find that finance's bread is buttered by the preservation of existing wealth and asserting the interests of the wealthy politically.

At the beginning of the 21st century, neoliberal policies were in their pomp and accelerated the rolling back of financial regulation so that markets were focused on maximizing the capacity of finance's 'wealth creators' to optimize their returns. The outcomes of these policies have been very different, however. Rather than seeking to maximize returns, investors instead looked to minimize the risk to their capital over the long term. There is more money in the world than ever before but, recalling Miles Jupp, 'most of it is tied up in land'. Capital preservation products drove growth in advisers whose specialisms were not access to primary markets for capital for businesses but instead the complex business of inheritance, family trusts and tax 'efficiency'.

This did not just extend to the investment industry, but was also a perhaps unintended consequence of the tightening of bank lending regulation following the financial crisis. Even prior to 2008, banks had been retreating from 'risky' lending categories, such as businesses in the real economy, driven by the cost of holding capital against the value of those assets which made them less profitable than, for example, lending on residential property. As a result, studies from both the Bank of England itself and activist organizations such as Positive Money showed that just 15 per cent of bank lending assets were from 'productive investment' and the rest was attributable to property, financial assets and other forms of investment.

As highlighted previously, Rishi Sunak, Chancellor of the Exchequer in 2021, identified while an MP the problem of a lack of capital investment by SMEs. When compared to other countries, such as the USA and Germany, this lack of investment explained the slow progress on the increase in productivity among companies that made up 50 per cent of the UK economy. Sunak proposed a radical solution in the form of new 'national savings bonds' for small businesses. Low productivity due to underinvestment is a major potential contributing factor to the stagnant growth in wages and overall 'incomes' of UK citizens since the beginning of this century. But who is going to take the risk on these types of businesses if banks are increasingly only able to provide low risk forms of working (or flexible) capital, and then only if you have significant collateral to put aside as security?

Fiscal policies were put into action, in the form of new tax incentives which encouraged and rewarded those who were prepared to put some of their capital at risk to support growth in the real economy. Initially, equity crowdfunding benefited from the existing incentives targeted at the venture capital fund industry, with investors qualifying for the Enterprise Investment Scheme (established in 1994) and, in 2012, the Seed Enterprise Investment Scheme which gave investors further tax relief on money invested in high risk start-up companies. P2P loans and debt-based securities issued by investment crowdfunding platforms were made eligible for the other flagship savings incentive from the UK government, such as the Innovative Finance ISA in 2016, which brought a new wave of investors providing debt finance for SMEs and also green and socially positive projects.

Finally, Social Investment Tax Relief was introduced by the UK government in 2014 to encourage investment into social enterprises, charities and community businesses that are committed to achieving a high impact social mission. The evidence is that investors do value these schemes as a way for them to put a percentage of their capital to work in the real economy and mitigate some of the risk of doing so (and to keep more of the rewards). Each of these schemes has been successful in encouraging money towards 'productive investment' targeted at businesses and project across the UK who otherwise would struggle to raise funding through institutional funds (either being too small or simply not having been to the right school).

The development of CMIs (which currently do not qualify for any tax incentive) was designed to allow investment in the real economy for those who were unable or not attracted to the prospect of higher risk, potentially higher return investments (or unable to benefit from the full effects of the tax reliefs in some cases). Backed by the covenant and protections of local councils (which technically cannot go bankrupt) these relatively low risk investments targeted 'green' and 'recovery' projects in West Berkshire and Warrington, with many more UK councils gearing up to follow suit and drive investment into local net zero projects. CMIs, by allowing more direct local investment in the regeneration of local communities for a competitive return, offer an alternative to the ideas outlined by Rishi Sunak in 2021 for money to be raised through national institutions such as National Savings & Investments (NS&Is).[18]

If we are going to mobilize money to support the recovery from the COVID-19 pandemic and the climate crisis of the next decades, we will need radically to address the problem of incentives in the finance industry pushing money 'uphill' rather than trickling down to the real economy.

Beyond the crisis of finance: crowdfunding versus cryptocurrencies

In 2009, Satoshi Nakamoto published a short paper entitled 'Bitcoin: A Peer to Peer Electronic Cash System'. Since the first Bitcoin was mined, the value of the coins in circulation has yo-yoed in value from US$0.0008 cents for the first Bitcoin to more than US$50,000 per Bitcoin at the time of writing (or rather, of Elon Musk tweeting). It is now estimated to be on its fifth bubble.

As an investment, then, it has been a wild ride. As money, or at least as a currency, despite some wild claims about acceptance, it is still rather a niche way to buy, or perhaps more accurately to 'swap' for, things. Although, as the journalist Hugo Rifkind relates, having bought some Bitcoins early in its history for 'research', it can produce some interesting outcomes – such as the realization that his daughter's bed had been purchased with a Bitcoin that was then worth £40 but which was suddenly worth somewhere in the region of £27,000.[19] But as Rifkind points out, and as we have argued in this book, the real question we should be examining is not the function of blockchains, hash and code, but what purpose Bitcoin brings to our money. To paraphrase Rifkind's take, what is the political project here, and why should we care?

As to Satoshi Nakamoto's motivations, we only have what he, she or they wrote in the original paper, as the identity of the originator of Bitcoin is unknown and subject to extensive internet speculation and conspiracy theories. The motivation in the paper is clear, which is to create a form of money that is no longer dependent on trust (and therefore the need for a third party to adjudicate or enforce that trust). Writing in 2009, during the last 'great financial crash', Nakamoto can be forgiven for worrying about the end of money, given that it was sufficiently scary to make all the world leaders head to the Excel Conference Centre in London's Docklands to 'save the world' (in the words of then prime minister, Gordon Brown).

Bitcoin, therefore, is another vision of society, one in which you only need to trust yourself and the 'math'. We are not sure how the real 'Nakamoto' would make the movie of Bitcoin so far, which seems to be something akin to 'Wolf of Wall Street meets The Road', but despite the underlying techno-anarchist narrative, it is still reliant on a human-based belief system to maintain its value. As the economist Frances Coppola wrote in an article for *Coindesk*:

> When faith rules the roost, people believe all sorts of incredible things. Bitcoin replacing the dollar as the global reserve currency is such an incredible thing. The chances of it happening seem very small. But as long as Bitcoin's supporters continue to believe that it is destined to rule the world, Bitcoin will have value; others can

benefit from that value even if they don't share the belief. Thanks to the faith of Bitcoin's true believers, Bitcoin will continue to be a good bet for investors.[20]

So, for Bitcoin's 'believers', it is a belief in the end of trust, thereby the end of money, and by extension the end of the world that keeps it going.

And yet, drawing on Yuval Noah Harari's book, *Sapiens: A Brief History of Humankind*, Bitcoin's vision is shown to be no different to other ways that humans have tried to co-operate, even if it is in a decidedly passive aggressive manner. Harari writes:

> This is exactly what I mean by an 'imagined order'. We believe in a particular order not because it is objectively true, but because believing in it enables us to cooperate effectively and forge a better society. Imagined orders are not evil conspiracies or useless mirages. Rather, they are the only way large numbers of human beings can cooperate effectively.

And he goes on:

> A natural order is a stable order. There is no chance that gravity will cease to function tomorrow, even if people stop believing in it. In contrast, an imagined order is always in danger of collapse, because it depends upon myths, and myths vanish once people stop believing in them. In order to safeguard an imagined order, continuous and strenuous efforts are imperative.[21]

Bitcoin is an attempt to create a sense of 'natural order' out of a belief system built on 'immutable' code. And why should we care? As we have outlined throughout this book, crowdfunding and P2P lending are not just a new form of FinTech, they are a response to a crisis of trust. That crisis is having far-reaching effects on not only our finance system but also democracy itself. The view of the crowdfunding innovator is an optimistic one, one which believes that democracy and society will benefit from creating more ways to trust and collaborate. In contrast, the Bitcoin view of democracy is more aligned with the rioters who invaded the US Congress in January 2021 than it is the vision of the US founding fathers, or even the Athenian founder of democracy, Kleisthenes.

To return to where we started at the beginning of the book, crisis literally means making a choice, a decision, taking a judgement on how we are to proceed. Two alternative futures for democratic finance currently present themselves, with a decision pending between a future either shaped by blockchains and Bitcoins or by crowdfunding and P2P finance. Each presents a very different way out of the current interregnum. One way forward is a 'rugged individualist' strategy for a world seemingly in retreat, going back to old ideas about money (mining for gold, value created by work, and so on), based on the belief that trust has fully collapsed. The other is about reinforcing existing networks of trust and building new ones, looking forward to new ways of moving money in order to change what it does, increasing the participation of more people in financial decision-making in pursuit of better outcomes for people and planet. We hope this book has gone some way to persuading you to follow the latter strategy.

CONCLUSION

The Change in Your Pocket

In recounting her experience of being asked the 'Bitcoin Question', Lana Swartz reveals that her response to friends and family enquiring about the risks of getting in on the cryptocurrency game is to ask what they want to achieve through their acquisition.[1] Simply put: what are all the Bitcoins for? The typical answers to Swartz's provocation are both achingly dull and easily anticipated. People have heard of others making decent returns by speculating on Bitcoin rallies and want to get in on the action. In other words, the primary motivation of those who want to acquire Bitcoins is to use them to acquire more Bitcoins, which at some point in the future will have risen to a price deemed high enough to 'cash out' via a fiat currency of choice. At the exit point of sale, after all, nobody imagines selling their Bitcoins for more Bitcoins.

The more imaginative would-be speculators answer in ways that reveal a growing sense of existential threat. As political, social and economic institutions lurch from one catastrophe to the next, at least they are providing a distraction from the impending world-ending breakdown of the climate. In short, if Bitcoin is to be the only non-institutionalized global currency within a matter of decades, doesn't it make sense to start hoarding them now?

In both responses, we can see the same instincts that drive people to save money. A desire to have more of it stored up against an uncertain future makes a good deal of sense from one point of view. But what is missing in the answers to Swartz's Bitcoin Question, and what we have been arguing for throughout this book, is any meaningful sense of the *purpose* of Bitcoin. As with mainstream finance, so much of the debate focuses upon the technical and functional possibilities of Bitcoin that we have failed sufficiently to pause and to reflect on what the advocates and users of Bitcoin are trying to achieve.

As we saw in Chapter Five, there is a reading of Bitcoin that would promote it – and the entire cryptocurrency and cryptoasset markets made possible by variations of DLTs[2] – as the way out of the current interregnum and towards a more democratic future. If the 'old Ruler' resembled a financial Leviathan – a single omnipotent entity, constituted of many individual parts yet behaving like a capricious sovereign ruler inspiring fear in its subjects and indifferent to the suffering it causes – then a libertarian 'Crypto Future' would splinter it into a thousand pieces and scatter it to the winds. If, as Swartz insists, all money is a bet on the future, then it is also a summoning up of a particular future. To paraphrase Marie Ekeland from Chapter Four, 'you're not just following the wind, you're making it blow'.

And yet, we also learn from Swartz that Bitcoin is a forestalling of the future, *preventing* a way out of the present interregnum. The logic of 'crypto' is one of deferral. Those who hold Bitcoin are always inclined to continue to do so. No matter how high the price climbs, the injunction is *not* to sell. Keep holding out waiting for a still higher price, a more distant future. Your big win? Well, it's always just around the next corner. Bitcoin's future is a receding horizon, either chasing the sun because the world suddenly seems so dark, or else trying to prevent the moment at which inflationary pressures start to alter the value of the investment. Our point here is that, if the ultimate success of Bitcoin is the end of currencies, then what are the holders of Bitcoin going to exchange Bitcoin for in order to realize its apparent market value? Also, if Bitcoin is intended one day to be used directly in the exchange of goods or services – as announced by the 'Technoking of Tesla' himself, Elon Musk, in March 2021,[3] before being hastily revoked two months later – then at what point does inflation start to play a role in the value of the investment? After all, the purpose of inflation in the present mainstream economy is to discourage the hoarding of cash (or other forms of 'script'), and yet, at least today, hoarding Bitcoins seems to be their primary (indeed only) real purpose.

Against this particular vision for a more 'democratic' finance, we have argued that crowdfunding and P2P finance provide an alternative way out of the interregnum that is less about retreat and more about the empowerment of 'the crowd' to make decisions on matters that concern them all. Indeed, as we saw in Chapter Three, this better reflects the original meaning of democracy as a form of life of *agora* – that intermediate space which connects the two other sectors of the *polis*, namely *ecclesia* (public, civic) and *oikos* (household). In an ancient city-state like Athens, Zygmunt Bauman reminds us, *agora* was a physical space to which the *boulē* (council) summoned several times each month all of the citizens (heads of *oikos*) to deliberate and decide upon the issues of joint and shared interests – and so to elect, or to draw by lots, its members.[4]

For obvious reasons, such a procedure could not be sustained once the body politic grew far beyond the borders of a city. It was unfeasible for all citizens to meet physically, and so *agora* could no longer mean, literally, a public square in which all citizens could be present in order to participate in the decision-making process. But that fact did not mean, Bauman maintains, that the true purpose underlying the establishment of the *agora* needed to be forever abandoned. Rather, as we have intimated in our own story, the history of democracy can be narrated as a series of successive efforts to keep both the purpose and its pursuit alive even after the disappearance of its physical possibilities. In short, instead of abandoning the principle of *agora* altogether, new ways need to be found for bringing the people together to have their say on the type of future they want to build.

In Chapter One, we outlined three models of democracy that we hoped would be instructive for helping the reader to assess how far crowdfunding can be seen as contributing to a democratization of finance. As a reminder, the first criteria was drawn from a *Representative/Aggregative* model and concerned crowdfunding's capacity *to overcome the distance between people and decision-making power.* The second criteria, adapted from a *Participatory/Deliberative* model, was the extent to which crowdfunding is transparently inclusive of more than just the usual White, male and retired group of 'sophisticated' investors such that *different people are enabled to hold significant power in determining outcomes from moving their money.* The third criteria, developed out of a *Radical/Agonistic* model, concerned how far crowdfunding is able *to disrupt the power of entrenched elites and offer an alternative way for civil society to decide upon the various competing ways that it may choose to provision what it collectively needs.*

As we have stated throughout this book, the current mainstream financial system can be seen as akin to a *Representative/Aggregative* model, with all of its attendant problems. The distance between citizens and the authority of real decision-making power typically leaves professional financiers (just as with elected politicians) far too unaccountable for their actions, despite the ability to switch banks and financial products. As with politicians, why switch if all that's on offer is basically more of the same? And as with our voting preferences so too with our financial behaviour, as we habitually hand over power to the same organizations we always have out of loyalty, habit or disinterest. In so doing, we continue to empower an elite to take decisions that we are left to hope will represent our best interests, or at least those of an aggregate well-being of the population. Crowdfunding dramatically closes this distance and invites us to take our own agency seriously when it comes to who we elect to lend to or invest with. Instead of empowering a distant financial elite to make investment decisions that impact the world we inhabit now and will in the future, we the people decide which projects to support and which outcomes best align with our values and our hopes for people and planet.

In this way, crowdfunding is currently closest to the participatory model of democracy as it heeds to the wisdom of multiple voices from different communities of interest who are invited to participate in the decision-making process of who and what gets funded. In this way, crowdfunding can help to deliver fairer, more inclusive and more sustainable outcomes by empowering people to disrupt and thus alter the destination of money. With the *Participatory/Deliberative* model based upon ideas of 'the public' and the 'common good', so too crowdfunding obviously privileges the collective wisdom of 'the crowd', guided by a sense that a plurality of perspectives are better at deciding which projects get funded and which do not. Through collective discussion, receipt of greater information and the opportunity to learn what others think and value – as often facilitated by online investor forums provided by platforms themselves, or else operating in independent spaces online – investors old and new can deliberate and have their voices heard.

There is a long way to go, of course. While crowdfunding as a model facilitates these participatory processes far better than mainstream finance, and often provides extremely low minimum investment thresholds with the aim of being socially inclusive, the UK and global markets remain largely dominated by White men over 55 years of age and retired. There is evidence that women and young people participate more freely in crowdfunding and P2P finance than they do in mainstream savings and investment products, but the market still remains short of being truly inclusive. And this matters since these more marginal voices need not only to be heard but to be influential in financial decision-making processes that shape the world we all inhabit.

Finally, we return to the account of Fred L. Block – one of the pioneers of 'democratic finance' – in assessing the extent to which crowdfunding provides a radical alternative to the financial Leviathan that has become so bloated during four decades of neoliberalism. Whereas, at the more *Radical/Agonistic* end of our democratic models, we find the 'Crypto Future' advocated by tech-utopians, in Block's assessment our radicalism ought instead to be directed towards reorganizing finance in such a way as to disempower the existing financial elite, not to plan for the complete collapse of all democratic systems and institutions. As a reminder, Block explains that the power of professional financiers stems from the deliberate construction of a financial system that requires the vast majority of private savings and investments to pass through mainstream financial institutions, such as high-street banks, pension funds and so on, enabling them to extract rents, transaction and handling fees, and a range of other micro-payments that collectively add up to trillions of dollars. As an investigation by the UK's FCA revealed in June 2017, the profit margins of asset managers in particular surpass those of the sectors in which they invest by a considerable margin.[5]

As such, one of the most radical and disruptive acts to that mainstream system is to change the flow of money by redirecting it into new and alternative financial channels that not only subvert the ability of professional financiers to extract those rents, but that also changes the destination of money by allowing citizens to privilege investment in the public infrastructure we all need and that the mainstream system has been unwilling or incapable of delivering for close to half a century. Only in this way, to deploy Block's own words once more, can we hope to 'open the path for the construction of a different kind of economy that would enhance the power of local communities, put greater emphasis on equality and social inclusion, and prioritize significant movement towards environmental sustainability'.[6]

Crowdfunding and P2P finance are demonstrable examples of exactly these new types of financial channels, as the case studies throughout this book have shown. How radical this becomes, and how capable it is of delivering genuinely progressive systemic change, will depend upon crowdfunding's capacity to address the ongoing issue of greater inclusivity and participation. In time, we suggest that crowdfunding as a form of democratic finance can point to a way out of the present interregnum that puts the power over money back into the hands of the people and lets them decide how best to use it in service of society and the environment.

To return to where we began, taken in its literal etymological meaning, the *crisis* of finance requires each of us now to make a judgement. While there are those with powerful vested interests in continuing to advocate for the 'old Ruler' as our best way out of the present interregnum, marshalling their forces to protect a financial Leviathan that seeks still greater distance from democratic control and accountability, we believe that the crisis demands one of two potential futures are now chosen.

One future privileges a radical decentralization driven by DLTs that would do away with the apparently crumbling 'legacy' institutions of popular democracies and modern economies, instead empowering a faceless network of code-literate authorizers and approvers situated around the world and with sufficient computer power to administer the lives of every human being on the planet. Whether that is the catalyst for, or the consequence of, new forms of authoritarianism founded upon an extreme libertarian ideology remains to be seen.[7] But in that future, money has no real purpose beyond its own accumulation and thus as an exercise of power over others. Another future, the one we advocate, points to a more civic form of finance that has the potential radically to repurpose money through reprising its role as a system of mutual trust for the collective provisioning of the things we all need by scaling up existing structures of crowdfunding and P2P finance.

Whichever decision we now make, one thing that both potential futures demonstrate is the importance of challenging mainstream finance through a great refusal of its own myths and stories. Mainstream economics still likes to think of itself not as a social science, but as a version of natural science. Its most dominant academic journals are bursting with refined causal models, quantifications and equations of all kinds, with the value of numbers frequently assigned far greater importance than the value of humans. In part, this is a consequence of a long-held obsession with mirroring the theoretical and methodological tools of physics.[8] What is more typically overlooked, however, is how the myths and stories that sustain mainstream economics share a long-held affinity with biology. Finance, for example, likes to imagine itself as an unfolding evolutionary process that cannot be stopped. With its faith placed firmly in those apparently 'invisible hands' of the market, finance positions itself as little more than a witness to an apparently natural evolution that it cannot possibly control. And, as with evolutionary processes in the natural world, so too finance likes to imagine that it has been somehow divinely ordained. Not willing to interfere with the apparent will of either deities or natural laws, finance strives only to manage and temper those processes through occasional and reluctant tweaks to its evolutionary unfurling.

As powerful as this story has become, there are no divine or natural laws at work. Finance is not some evolution of a natural or biological entity following its own internal teleological path. To paraphrase Yuval Noah Harari, just like gods in the universe, nations, money, human rights, laws and justice – so finance too does not exist outside the common imagination of human beings. Finance is a system built by human beings upon a system of mutual trust that we have chosen to call 'money', and thus it is entirely shaped by social relations. As such, it is capable of being reshaped by those same human beings in order to provision right now the things that people need for a good life in harmony with the natural world. Crowdfunding is one of the ways that we can start to tell a new story about money, one that puts people at the centre of financial decision-making and in turn takes a chance to reinvigorate democracy.

All you have to do is to recognize the change in your pocket.

Notes

one The Crisis of Finance

1 Roitman (2012; 2013).
2 Walby (2015), p 8.
3 Ghosh (2017), Klein (2015; 2019), Pettifor (2020), Urry (2011).
4 Crouch (2000), Norris (2010).
5 Bauman (2013), Blakeley (2019), Dorling (2015; 2019).
6 Bauman (2010; 2012), Bordoni (2016).
7 Babic (2020), Gramsci (1971), p 276.
8 Bauman (2017).
9 Davis (2020).
10 Wolf (2020).
11 Fisher (2020).
12 According to *Forbes Magazine*, there were just over 550 billionaires in the world in 2004. By 2020, there were estimated to be 2,095. https://www.forbes.com/billionaires/, accessed 7 February 2021.
13 Assets under management (AUM) is the total market value of the investments that a person or entity handles on behalf of other investors.
14 https://www.pwc.com/gx/en/industries/financial-services/asset-management/publications/asset-wealth-management-revolution-2020.html, summarized here: https://www.pwc.com/gx/en/industries/financial-services/assets/wealth-management-2-0-data-tool/pwc_awm_revolution_2020.pdf, both accessed 26 March 2021.
15 https://www.thinkingaheadinstitute.org/research-papers/the-worlds-largest-asset-managers-2020/, accessed 18 March 2021. The figure of $650 billion is an unofficial estimate provided by FCA research based upon a survey of revenues and costs for UK industry. Potential ranges are from $500 billion to $750 billion. Significantly, the FCA's own report in 2017 highlighted that the estimated margins of asset managers averaged more than 38 per cent, which is far greater than the industries in which their customers' money is invested. As the FCA report concedes, precise figures are hard to obtain as the industry claims not to maintain records of individual fund costs and profitability. Our intention here is to point to the likely size of the revenues, not to provide that precise figure.
16 Davis and Walsh (2017), Fine (2013), Lapavistas (2011), Masso et al (2020), Sawyer (2013), Van Der Zwan (2019).
17 CCAF (2020).
18 Jacobsen (2019).

[19] Short selling is a fairly simple concept. An investor borrows a stock, sells the stock, and then buys the stock back to return it to the lender. Short sellers are betting that the stock they sell will drop in price.

[20] A short squeeze occurs when a stock or other asset jumps sharply higher, forcing traders who had bet that its price would fall to buy it in order to forestall even greater losses. Their scramble to buy only adds to the upward pressure on the stock's price.

[21] https://www.ft.com/content/c219df22-0d93-34d7-a729-5a7928abb460, accessed 17 March 2021.

[22] https://www.allianceofdemocracies.org/initiatives/the-copenhagen-democracy-summit/the-summit-2021/, accessed 18 March 2021.

[23] https://www.nytimes.com/2021/02/04/world/europe/italy-mario-draghi.html, accessed 24 February 2021.

[24] https://www.theguardian.com/money/us-money-blog/2014/aug/11/women-rights-money-timeline-history, accessed 18 March 2021.

[25] https://makemymoneymatter.co.uk/, accessed 18 March 2021.

[26] Davis and Cartwright (2019); Davis (2021). https://www.abundanceinvestment.com/how-it-works/about-municipal-investments; https://baumaninstitute.leeds.ac.uk/research/cmis-local-climate-bonds/; https://baumaninstitute.leeds.ac.uk/research/financing-for-society/; and https://pcancities.org.uk/report-community-municipal-bonds-turning-words-action, all accessed 18 March 2021. See also: https://www.greenfinanceinstitute.co.uk/local-climate-bonds-a-cost-effective-way-to-raise-billions-for-councils-green-plans-says-new-campaign/, accessed 11 August 2021.

[27] Haldane (2021).

[28] We wish to thank Katy Wright at the University of Leeds for her assistance in helping us to imagine and describe these three models of democracy, which draw upon her work on civic participation and community resilience (Wright 2021).

[29] For example, the International Covenant on Civil and Political Rights (1976: Article 25) and the Declaration of the Right to Development (1986: Paragraph 1 Article 1).

[30] https://www.thersa.org/reports/artificial-intelligence-real-public-engagement, accessed 23 January 2021.

[31] Examples include: https://www.leedsclimate.org.uk/leeds-climate-change-citizens-jury; and https://www.edinburghclimate.org.uk/, accessed 28 October 2020.

[32] Matten and Crane (2005), p 7.

[33] https://www.bbc.co.uk/programmes/m000py8t. At the time of writing, all four 2020 Reith Lectures were also available to be viewed via the

BBC's iPlayer service (worldwide restrictions may apply outside of the UK). See also Carney (2021).

[34] Carney (2021), King (2016).

[35] https://www.ft.com/content/f92b6c67-15ef-460f-8655-e458f2fe2487, accessed 18 March 2021.

[36] Bruff and Tansel (2019), Davies (2014), Harvey (2005).

two What is Crowdfunding?

[1] Differences in the evolution of the definition and regulation of P2P lending require the broader nomenclature of P2P finance when describing the market as it is today.

[2] https://www.zopa.com/, accessed 15 December 2020.

[3] Securitization is the packaging of the rights to the cash flows of a large number of debt-based financial assets in aggregate. The value of these 'securities' is based on the risk and default rates of the underlying loans or bonds.

[4] Baeck et al (2012), p 3.

[5] Reiser and Dean (2017), Borst et al (2018).

[6] Davis and Braunholtz-Speight (2016), Langley (2016), Ahlers et al (2015), Cholakova and Clarysse (2015).

[7] https://www.crowdfunder.co.uk/; https://www.spacehive.com/, accessed 15 December 2020.

[8] These rule changes in 2019 were in part the result of research led by Mark Davis with both the Cambridge Centre for Alternative Finance (CCAF) and the FCA. See Davis et al (2020).

[9] https://www.abundanceinvestment.com/; https://www.fundingcircle.com/uk/; https://www.zopa.com/, accessed 15 December 2020.

[10] https://www.crowdcube.com/; https://www.seedrs.com/, accessed 15 December 2020.

[11] https://www.ethex.org.uk/, accessed 15 December 2020.

[12] The regulatory framework for crowdfunding was created in 2014 and revised in 2019. See also note 8 in this chapter.

[13] Angerer et al (2017), Belleflamme et al (2014), Lehner (2013), Mollick (2014).

[14] Davis et al (2020).

[15] Bone et al (2019).

[16] Mirowski (2013), Tooze (2018).

[17] Aitken (2006), Langley and Leyshon (2017), Maurer (2008), Nelms et al (2018), Tooker and Clarke (2018).

[18] Each of these global region reports are freely available here: https://www.jbs.cam.ac.uk/faculty-research/centres/alternative-finance/publications/, accessed 17 December 2020.

[19] CCAF (2020): https://www.jbs.cam.ac.uk/faculty-research/centres/alternative-finance/publications/the-global-alternative-finance-market-benchmarking-report/, accessed 17 December 2020.

[20] https://www.ukcfa.org.uk/; https://www.innovatefinance.com/36hgroup/; https://www.ukbaa.org.uk/, accessed 15 December 2020.

[21] https://www.compassonline.org.uk/; https://financeinnovationlab.org/; https://www.ippr.org/; https://makemymoneymatter.co.uk/; https://neweconomics.org/; https://neweconomyorganisers.org/; https://positivemoney.org/; https://shareaction.org/; https://www.taxjustice.net/, accessed 15 December 2020.

[22] https://www.osborneclarke.com/insights/the-regulation-of-crowdfunding-in-the-uk/, accessed 19 March 2021.

[23] FCA (2017), p 6.

[24] See p 9 of this book.

[25] Categorization and Appropriateness were added to the regulatory framework for investment based crowdfunding in 2014 and for P2P lending (36H) in 2019. Categorization refers to the self-certification by investors of their investment experience to ensure potential customers are aware of the need to understand the risks of the investment. The new category of 'Restricted Retail', in which investors undertake not to invest more than 10 per cent of their net investible assets, was created to highlight the additional risks of investing in 'unlisted' or 'non-readily realizable' securities versus publicly listed stocks. Investors can also self-certify as 'sophisticated/experienced' investors or as 'High Net Worth' investors, which does not change their status in terms of recourse to complaint but that does allow them to consider investing larger proportions of their investible assets.

[26] https://assets.publishing.service.gov.uk/government/uploads/system/uploads/attachment_data/file/945247/Gloster_Report_FINAL.pdf, accessed 24 November 2020.

[27] https://www.economist.com/international/2013/05/18/breaking-ground, accessed 30 September 2020.

[28] Block (2014), p 4.

[29] Block (2014), p 11.

[30] Lewis (1989) cited in La Berge (2015), p 82.

[31] Gibson-Graham et al (2013), Gibson-Graham (1996; 2006).

[32] Bone et al (2019), Floyd et al (2015).

[33] Lawrence (2014), Walby (2013).

[34] Prabhakar (2021).

[35] Cox et al (2014), Greenham et al (2013), Wright (2021).

[36] Goulden et al (2014), Hall et al (2016).

[37] Davis et al (2020).

three Democratic Finance, Then and Now

1 Brown (2015; 2019), Crouch (2011), Mirowski (2013).

2 Mellor (2016), p 20.

3 https://www.thisismoney.co.uk/money/news/article-7759277/Total-household-net-wealth-surges-14trillion-stash-cash-pensions-property.html, accessed 15 March 2021. In 2020 the value of the UK's retirement wealth, for example, surpassed that of the value of its residential property wealth for the first time.

4 These bailouts involved nation states owning shares in their major banking institutions and providing cash to fill the holes in their balance sheets. These holes were left by the explosion of the value of loans and investments, which had previously been seen as rock solid and built on 'bricks and mortar' assets.

5 Simply put, QE involved the purchase of billions of dollars, euros and pounds worth of government debt from financial institutions to shore up the stock markets.

6 https://www.theguardian.com/business/2017/aug/09/alistair-darling-rbs-said-they-would-run-out-of-money-in-early-afternoon, accessed 4 March 2021.

7 Bauman and Rovirosa-Madrazo (2010), p 21.

8 Bauman and Rovirosa-Madrazo (2010), p 22.

9 Plato (c.375 BCE).

10 Christophers (2020).

11 Excerpt from p 7 of the second lecture transcript, BBC Reith Lectures 2020: https://downloads.bbc.co.uk/radio4/reith2020/Reith_2020_Lecture_2_transcript.pdf, accessed 19 March 2021.

12 Excerpt from p 12 of the first lecture transcript, BBC Reith Lectures 2020: https://downloads.bbc.co.uk/radio4/reith2020/Reith_2020_Lecture_1_transcript.pdf, accessed 24 March 2021.

13 Schofield (2006), p 258.

14 Keynes (1936), Samuelson and Nordhaus (1948).

15 https://www.theguardian.com/business/2008/oct/24/economics-creditcrunch-federal-reserve-greenspan, accessed 26 May 2020.

16 https://foreignpolicy.com/2020/05/13/european-central-bank-myth-monetary-policy-german-court-ruling/, accessed 19 March 2021.

17 Solon was a blend of a religious and a political leader in pre-democracy Athens.

18 Bauman (2000; 2005; 2007).

19 Millett (1991).

20 Frontispiece to Millet (1991), emphasis added.

21 Graeber (2011).

22 Foster (1967), p 214.

23 Hart (1986). See also Hart (2000) and https://thememorybank.co.uk/keith/, accessed 26 May 2021.

24 Slater (2018).

25 Adjusting for inflation this equates to £240 million in today's prices (assuming a 1.6 per cent inflation rate). See https://www.bankofengland.co.uk/monetary-policy/inflation/inflation-calculator, accessed 26 March 2021.

26 Threadneedle Street is famous as the site of the Bank of England in London, UK. The bank itself is sometimes colloquially known as 'the Old Lady of Threadneedle Street' and has been based at its current location since 1734. The London Stock Exchange was also situated on Threadneedle Street until 2004, when it relocated to nearby Paternoster Square.

27 https://www.cps.org.uk/files/reports/original/171116092827-ANewEraforRetailBonds.pdf, accessed 26 March 2021.

28 https://makemymoneymatter.co.uk/, accessed 18 March 2021.

29 https://green-party.medium.com/climate-covid-and-care-a-budget-for-critical-times-d9ab306aaaa4, accessed 18 March 2021.

four The Destination of Money

1 https://sifted.eu/articles/marie-ekeland-2050/, accessed 24 February 2021.

2 Mazzucato (2021), p 16.

3 Piketty (2014; 2020).

4 https://www.bankofengland.co.uk/speech/2016/enabling-the-fintech-transformation-revolution-restoration-or-reformation, accessed 19 March 2021.

5 https://positivemoney.org/2020/03/positive-money-leads-call-for-new-bank-of-england-governor-to-step-up-climate-action/, accessed 26 May 2020.

6 Chang (2010).

7 Mellor (2019), p 6.

8 Wittgenstein (1921).

9 Earle et al (2017). See also: https://www.rethinkeconomics.org/, accessed 16 March 2020.

10 Weber (1922; 1946).

11 Marx (1859; 1867).

12 https://www.bankofengland.co.uk/speech/2019/mark-carney-speech-at-the-mansion-house-bankers-and-merchants-dinner, accessed 19 March 2021.

13 www.margaretthatcher.org/document/105454, accessed 4 March 2021.

14 https://www.ftserussell.com/products/indices/ftse4good, accessed 2 July 2021.

15 https://jpm.pm-research.com/content/1/1/88, accessed 19 March 2021.

16 https://lareviewofbooks.org/article/a-dollar-is-a-dollar-is-not-a-dollar-unmasking-the-social-and-moral-meanings-of-money/, accessed 2 July 2021.

17 Sanne (2002), p 273.

18 Evans (2009), p 1029.

19 Zelizer (2005; 2012); Bandeli (2012).

20 Zelizer (1994).

21 Malinowski (1922).

22 Hart (1986), Mauss (1954). See also https://thememorybank.co.uk/keith/, accessed 26 May 2020.

23 Hart (2014), p 42.

24 Kelton (2020)

25 Kelton (2020), pp 20–3.

26 Mazzucato (2013).

27 Christophers (2020).

28 Mazzucato (2018).

29 Mazzucato (2021).

30 Mazzucato (2021), p 8.

31 Mazzucato (2021), p 206.

32 https://www.spacex.com/, accessed 19 March 2021.

33 https://www.bbc.co.uk/news/science-environment-55564448, accessed 19 March 2021.

34 This statement is often attributed to the Slovenian philosopher Slavoj Žižek, via Mark Fisher's book *Capitalist Realism* (2009). Matthew Beaumont (2014) usefully notes that the idea is more likely to come from Frederic Jameson and H. Bruce Franklin.

five Futures of Democratic Finance

1 https://www.opendemocracy.net/en/oureconomy/washington-consensus-dead-what-should-replace-it/, accessed 19 March 2021.

2 Lawrence (2014), Walby (2013).

3 Chao et al (2020)

4 https://www.bankofengland.co.uk/letter/2021/march/mpc-remit-2021, accessed 19 March 2021.

5 https://www.theguardian.com/uk-news/2021/mar/03/environmental-groups-not-convinced-by-sunaks-green-growth-budget, accessed 4 March 2021.

6   https://robinhood.com/us/en/; https://tikr.com/; https://bigexchange. com/, accessed 22 March 2021.

7   Quigley (2019). See also: https://corpgov.law.harvard.edu/2021/03/01/ an-introduction-to-activist-stewardship/, accessed 4 March 2021.

8   Bauman (2000), Beck (1992).

9   https://www.reddit.com/t/gamestop/, accessed 7 March 2021.

10 Bourdieu (2005), p 209.

11 Walby (2015), pp 144–60.

12 Falk and Maenpaa (1999).

13 Weiner (1992).

14 Appadurai (1988).

15 Polanyi (1944).

16 https://www.youtube.com/watch?v=PquBmjlS4uI, accessed 19 March 2021.

17 https://www.youtube.com/watch?v=lAPcXc5ysZ0, accessed 19 March 2021.

18 https://www.nsandi.com/, accessed 19 March 2021.

19 https://www.thetimes.co.uk/article/bitcoins-political-project-has-failed-dismally-8565763ld, accessed 19 March 2021.

20 https://www.coindesk.com/why-bitcoin-thrives-wont-replace-dollar, accessed 19 March 2021.

21 Both quotes from Harari (2015), p 124.

Conclusion: The Change in Your Pocket

1   https://www.noemamag.com/bitcoin-as-a-meme-and-a-future/, accessed 25 March 2021.

2   DuPont (2019), Vigna and Casey (2018).

3   https://www.theguardian.com/technology/2021/mar/15/elon-musk-changes-his-tesla-job-title-to-technoking; https://www.nytimes.com/ 2021/03/24/business/elon-musk-tesla-bitcoin.html, both accessed 25 March 2021.

4   Bauman (2011), pp 10–11.

5   https://www.fca.org.uk/publication/market-studies/ms15-2-3.pdf, accessed 25 March 2021. Among the reports key findings, the FCA notes: 'We confirm our interim finding that there is considerable price clustering on the asset management charge for retail funds, and active charges have remained broadly stable over the last 10 years. We agree with respondents who said that, in and of themselves, price clustering and broadly stable prices do not necessarily mean that prices are above their competitive level. However, we also found high levels of profitability, with average profit margins of 36% for the firms we sampled. Firms' own

evidence to us also suggested they do not typically lower prices to win new business. These factors combined indicate that price competition is not working as effectively as it could be.'

[6] Block (2014), p 11.

[7] Brown (2019), Bruff and Tansel (2019).

[8] Chang (2014).

References

Ahlers, G.K.C., Cumming, D., Günther, C. and Schweizer, D. (2015) 'Signalling in Equity Crowdfunding', *Entrepreneurship Theory and Practice*, 39, 4: pp 955–80.

Aitken, R. (2006) 'Capital at Its Fringes', *New Political Economy*, 11, 4: pp 479–98.

Angerer, M., Brem, A., Kraus, S. and Peter, A. (2017) 'Start-up Funding via Equity Crowdfunding in Germany: A Qualitative Analysis of Success Factors', *The Journal of Entrepreneurial Finance*, 19, 1: pp 1–34.

Appadurai, A. (1988) *The Social Life of Things: Commodities in Cultural Perspective*. Cambridge: Cambridge University Press.

Babic, M. (2020) 'Let's Talk about the Interregnum: Gramsci and the Crisis of the Liberal World Order', *International Affairs*, 96, 3: pp 767–86.

Baeck, P., Collins, L. and Westlake, S. (2012) *Crowding In: How the UK's Businesses, Charities, Government and Financial System Can Make the Most of Crowdfunding*. London: Nesta.

Bandelj, N. (2012) 'Relational Work and Economic Sociology', *Politics and Society*, 40, 2: pp 175–201.

Bauman, Z. (2000) *Liquid Modernity*. Cambridge: Polity Press.

Bauman, Z. (2005) *Liquid Life*. Cambridge: Polity Press.

Bauman, Z. (2007) *Liquid Times: Living in an Age of Uncertainty*. Cambridge: Polity Press.

Bauman, Z. (2010) 'The Triple Challenge', in M. Davis and K. Tester (eds) *Bauman's Challenge: Sociological Issues for the 21st Century*. London: Palgrave, pp 200–5.

Bauman, Z. (2011) *Collateral Damages: Social Inequalities in a Global Age*. Cambridge: Polity.

Bauman, Z. (2012) 'Times of Interregnum', *Ethics and Global Politics*, 5, 1: pp 49–56.

Bauman, Z. (2013) *Does the Richness of the Few Benefit Us All?* Cambridge: Polity.

Bauman, Z. (2017) *Retrotopia*. Cambridge: Polity.

Bauman, Z. and Rovirosa-Madrazo, C. (2010) *Living on Borrowed Time*. Cambridge: Polity.

Beaumont, M. (2014) 'Imagining the End Times: Ideology, the Contemporary Disaster Movie, *Contagion*', in M. Flisfeder and L.P. Willis (eds) *Žižek and Media Studies*. New York: Palgrave, pp 79–89.

Beck, U. (1992) *Risk Society: Towards a New Modernity*. London: Sage.

Belleflamme, P., Lambert, T. and Schwienbacher, A. (2014) 'Crowdfunding: Tapping the Right Crowd', *Journal of Business Venturing*, 29, 5: pp 585–609.

Blakeley, G. (2019) *Stolen: How to Save the World from Financialisation*. London: Repeater Books.

Block, F.L. (2014) 'Democratic Finance', *Politics and Society*, 42, 1: pp 3–28.

Bone, J., Old, R., Baeck, P. and Boyle, D. (2019) *Taking Ownership: Community Empowerment through Crowdfunding Investment*. London: Nesta.

Bordoni C. (2016) *Interregnum: Beyond Liquid Modernity*. Bielefeld: Transcript.

Borst, I., Moser, C. and Ferguson, J. (2018) 'From Friendfunding to Crowdfunding: Relevance of Relationships, Social Media, and Platform Activities to Crowdfunding Performance', *New Media and Society*, 20, 4: pp 1396–414.

Bourdieu, P. (2005) *The Social Structures of the Economy*. Cambridge: Polity.

Brown, W. (2015) *Undoing the Demos: Neoliberalism's Stealth Revolution*. Cambridge, MA: Zone Books.

Brown, W. (2019) *In the Ruins of Neoliberalism: The Rise of Antidemocratic Politics in the West*. New York: Columbia University Press.

Bruff, I. and Tansel, C.B. (2019) 'Authoritarian Neoliberalism: Trajectories of Knowledge Production and Praxis', *Globalizations*, 16, 3: pp 233–44.

Carney, M. (2021) *Value(s): Building a Better World for All*. London: William Collins.

CCAF (2020) *The Global Alternative Finance Market Benchmarking Report*. Cambridge: Cambridge Centre for Alternative Finance.

Chang, H.-J. (2010) *23 Things They Don't Tell You About Capitalism*. London: Allen Lane.

Chang, H.-J. (2014) *Economics: The User's Guide*. London: Allen Lane/Pelican Books.

Chao, E.J., Serwaah, P., Baah-Peprah, P. and Shneor, R. (2020) 'Crowdfunding in Africa: Opportunities and Challenges', in R. Shneor, L. Zhao and B.-T. Flåten (eds) *Advances in Crowdfunding: Research and Practice*. London: Palgrave, pp 319–39.

Cholakova, M. and Clarysse, B. (2015) 'Does the Possibility to Make Equity Investments in Crowdfunding Projects Crowd Out Reward-Based Investments?', *Entrepreneurship Theory and Practice*, 39, 1: pp 145–72.

Christophers, B. (2020) *Rentier Capitalism: Who Owns the Economy, and Who Pays for It?* London: Verso.

Cox, E., Broadbridge, A. and Raikes, L. (2014) *Building Economic Resilience? An Analysis of Local Enterprise Partnerships' Plans*. Newcastle: IPPR North.

Crouch, C. (2000) *Post-Democracy*. Cambridge: Polity.

Crouch, C. (2011) *The Strange Non-Death of Neoliberalism*. Cambridge: Polity.

Davies, W. (2014) *The Limits of Neoliberalism: Authority, Sovereignty and the Logic of Competition*. London: Sage.

Davis, A. and Walsh, C. (2017) 'Distinguishing Financialization from Neoliberalism', *Theory, Culture & Society*, 34, 5–6: pp 27–51.

Davis, M. (2020) 'Hermeneutics contra Fundamentalism: Zygmunt Bauman's Method for Thinking in Dark Times', *Thesis Eleven*, 156, 1: pp 27–44.

Davis, M. (2021) *Community Municipal Investments: Accelerating the Potential of Local Net Zero Strategies*. Leeds: University of Leeds.

Davis, M. and Braunholtz-Speight, T. (2016) *Financial Innovation Today: Towards Economic Resilience*. York: Friends Provident Foundation.

Davis, M. and Cartwright, L. (2019) *Financing for Society: Assessing the Suitability of Crowdfunding for the Public Sector*. Leeds: University of Leeds.

Davis, M., Wardrop, R. and Braunholtz-Speight, T. (2020) 'Crowdfunding as Democratic Finance? Understanding How and Why UK Investors Trust These Markets', *Revista Internacional de Sociología*, 78, 4: e173.

Dorling, D. (2015) *Injustice: Why Social Inequality Still Persists*. Bristol: Policy Press.

Dorling, D. (2019) *Inequality and the 1%*. London: Verso.

DuPont, Q. (2019) *Crytpocurrencies and Blockchains*. Cambridge: Polity.

Earle, J., Moran, C. and Ward-Perkins, Z. (2017) *Econocracy: The Perils of Leaving Economics to the Experts*. London: Penguin/Random House.

Evans, M.S. (2009) 'Zelizer's Theory of Money and the Case of Local Currencies', *Environment and Planning A*, 41, 5: pp 1026–41.

Falk, P. and Maenpaa, P. (1999) *Hitting the Jackpot: Lives of Lottery Millionaires*. Oxford: Berg.

FCA (2017) *Our Mission 2017: How We Regulate Financial Services*. London: Financial Conduct Authority.

Fine, B. (2013) 'Financialization from a Marxist Perspective', *International Journal of Political Economy*, 42, 4: pp 47–66.

Fisher, M. (2009) *Capitalist Realism: Is There No Alternative?* London: Zero Books.

Fisher, P.G. (ed) (2020) *Making the Financial System Sustainable*. Cambridge: Cambridge University Press.

Floyd, D., Gregory, D. and Wilson, N. (2015) *After the Gold Rush: The Alternative Commission on Social Investment*. London: Esmée Fairburn Foundation.

Foster, G.M. (1967) *Tzintzuntzan: Mexican Peasants in a Changing World*. Boston: Little, Brown & Co.

Ghosh, A. (2017) *The Great Derangement: Climate Change and the Unthinkable*. Chicago: University of Chicago Press.

Gibson-Graham, J.K. (1996) *The End of Capitalism (As We Knew It): A Feminist Critique of Political Economy*. Oxford and Cambridge, MA: Blackwell Publishers.

Gibson-Graham, J.K. (2006) *A Postcapitalist Politics*. Minneapolis: University of Minnesota Press.

Gibson-Graham, J.K., Cameron, J. and Healy, S. (2013) *Take Back the Economy: An Ethical Guide for Transforming our Communities*. Minneapolis: University of Minnesota Press.

Goulden, M., Bedwell, B., Rennick-Egglestone, S., Rodden, T. and Spence, A. (2014) 'Smart Grids, Smart Users? The Role of the User in Demand Side Management', *Energy Research and Social Science*, 2: pp 21–9.

Graeber, D. (2011) *Debt: The First 5000 Years*. New York: Melville House.

Gramsci, A. (1971) *Selections from the Prison Notebooks*, ed and trans Q. Hoare and G. Nowell Smith. London: Lawrence & Wishart.

Greenham, T., Cox, E. and Ryan-Collins, J. (2013) *Mapping Economic Resilience*. York: Friends Provident Foundation.

Haldane, A. (2021) 'How to Remake Britain: Why We Need Community Capitalism', *New Statesman*, 17 March, https:// www.newstatesman.com/politics/devolution/2021/03/how-remake-britain-why-we-need-community-capitalism, accessed 26 March 2021.

Hall, S., Foxon, T.J. and Bolton, R. (2016) 'Financing the Civic Energy Sector: How Financial Institutions Affect Ownership Models in Germany and the United Kingdom', *Energy Research and Social Science*, 12: pp 5–15.

Harari, Y.N. (2015) *Sapiens: A Brief History of Humankind*. New York: Vintage.

Hart, K. (1986) 'Heads or Tails? Two Sides of the Coin', *Man*, 21, 4: pp 637–56.

Hart, K. (2014) 'Marcel Mauss's Economic Vision, 1920–25: Anthropology, Politics, Journalism', *Journal of Classical Sociology*, 14, 1: pp 34–44.

Hart, K. (2000) *The Memory Bank: Money in an Unequal World*. London: Profile Books.

Harvey, D. (2005) *A Brief History of Neoliberalism*. Oxford: Oxford University Press.

Jacobsen, M.H. (2019) 'Liquid-modern Emotions: Exploring Zygmunt Bauman's Contribution to the Sociology of Emotions', *Emotions and Society*, 1, 1: pp 99–116.

Kelton, S. (2020) *The Deficit Myth: Modern Monetary Theory and the Birth of the People's Economy*. London: Hachette/John Murray.

Keynes, J.M. [1936] (2017) *The General Theory of Employment, Interest, and Money*. London: Routledge/Macat Library.

King, M. (2016) *The End of Alchemy: Money, Banking and the Future of the Global Economy*. London: Little, Brown Book Group.

Klein, N. (2015) *This Changes Everything: Capitalism versus the Climate*. London: Penguin Books.

Klein, N. (2019) *On Fire: The Burning Case for a Green New Deal*. London: Penguin Books.

La Berge, L.C. (2015) *Scandals and Abstraction: Financial Fiction of the Long 1980s*. Oxford: Oxford University Press.

Langley, P. (2016) 'Crowdfunding in the United Kingdom: A Cultural Economy', *Economic Geography*, 92, 3: pp 301–21.

Langley, P. and Leyshon, A. (2017) 'Capitalizing on the Crowd: The Monetary and Financial Ecologies of Crowdfunding', *Environment and Planning A*, 49, 5: pp 1019–39.

Lapavitsas, C. (2011) 'Theorizing Financialization', *Work, Employment and Society*, 25, 4: pp 611–26.

Lawrence, M. (2014) *Definancialisation: A Democratic Reform of Finance*. London: IPPR.

Lehner, O.M. (2013) 'Crowdfunding Social Ventures: A Model and Research Agenda', *Venture Capital*, 15, 4: pp 289–311.

Lewis, M. (1989) *Liar's Poker*. New York: Penguin.

Malinowski, B. [1922] (2002) *Argonauts of the Western Pacific: An Account of Native Enterprise and Adventure in the Archipelagoes of Melanesian New Guinea*. London and New York: Routledge.

Marx, K. [1859] (1993) *A Contribution to the Critique of Political Economy*. Moscow: Progress Publishers.

Marx, K. [1867] (1990) *Capital: A Critique of Political Economy, Volume One*. London: Penguin.

Masso, M., Davis, M. and Albade, N. (2020) 'The Problematic Conceptualization of Financialization: Differentiating Causes, Consequences and Socio-Economic Actors' Financialized Behaviour', *Revista Internacional de Sociología*, 78, 4: e169.

Matten, D. and Crane, A. (2005) 'Corporate Citizenship: Toward an Extended Theoretical Conceptualization', *The Academy of Management Review*, 30, 1: pp 166–79.

Maurer, B. (2008) 'Resocializing Finance? Or Dressing It in Mufti?', *Journal of Cultural Economy*, 1, 1: pp 65–78.

Mauss, M. [1925] (2001) *The Gift: Forms and Functions of Exchange in Archaic Societies*. London: Routledge.

Mazzucato, M. (2013) *The Entrepreneurial State: Debunking Public vs. Private Sector Myths*. London: Anthem Press.

Mazzucato, M. (2018) *The Value of Everything: Making and Taking in the Global Economy*. London: Allen Lane.

Mazzucato, M. (2021) *The Mission Economy: A Moonshot Guide to Changing Capitalism*. London: Allen Lane.

Mellor, M. (2016) *Debt or Democracy: Public Money for Sustainability and Social Justice*. London: Pluto Press.

Mellor, M. (2019) *Money: Myths, Truths and Alternatives*. Bristol: Policy Press.

Millett, P. (1991) *Lending and Borrowing in Ancient Athens*. Cambridge: Cambridge University Press.

Mirowski, P. (2013) *Never Let a Serious Crisis Go to Waste: How Neoliberalism Survived the Financial Meltdown*. New York: Verso.

Mollick, E. (2014) 'The Dynamics of Crowdfunding: An Exploratory Study', *Journal of Business Venturing*, 29, 1: pp 1–16.

Nelms, T.C., Maurer, B., Swartz, L. and Mainwairing, S. (2018) 'Social Payments: Innovation, Trust, BitCoin and the Sharing Economy', *Theory, Culture and Society*, 35, 3: pp 13–33.

Norris, P. (2010) *Democratic Deficit: Critical Citizens Revisited*. Cambridge: Cambridge University Press.

Pettifor, A. (2020) *The Case for the Green New Deal*. London: Verso.

Piketty, T. (2014) *Capital in the Twenty-First Century*. Cambridge, MA: Harvard University Press.

Piketty, T. (2020) *Capital and Ideology*. Cambridge, MA: Harvard University Press.

Plato [c.375 BCE] (2007) *The Republic*. London: Penguin Classics Edition.

Polanyi, K. [1944] (2002) *The Great Transformation: The Political and Economic Origins of Our Time*. Boston: Beacon Press.

Prabhakar, R. (2021) *Financial Inclusion: Critique and Alternatives*. Bristol: Policy Press.

Quigley, E. (2019) 'Universal Ownership in the Anthropocene', *SSRN*, May 13, 2019, https://papers.ssrn.com/sol3/papers.cfm?abstract_id=3457205, accessed 18 March 2021.

Reiser, D.B. and Dean, S.A. (2017) *Social Enterprise Law*. Oxford: Oxford University Press.

Roitman, J. (2012) 'Crisis', http://www.politicalconcepts.org/roitman-crisis/, accessed 18 March 2021.

Roitman, J. (2013) *Anti-Crisis*. Durham, NC: Duke University Press.

Samuelson, P.A. and Nordhaus, W. (1948) *Economics*. New York: McGraw Hill.

Sanne, C. (2002) 'Willing Consumers—or Locked-in? Policies for a Sustainable Consumption', *Ecological Economics*, 42: pp 273–87.

Sawyer, M. (2013) 'What is Financialization?', *International Journal of Political Economy*, 42, 4: pp 5–18.

Schofield, M. (2006) *Plato: Political Philosophy*. Oxford: Oxford University Press.

Simmel, G. [1900] (2011) *The Philosophy of Money*. London: Routledge Classics.

Slater, M. (2018) *The National Debt: A Short History*. London: C Hurst & Co Publishers Ltd.

Smith, A. [1759] (2010) *The Theory of Moral Sentiments*. London: Penguin.

Smith, A. [1776] (1982) *An Inquiry into the Nature and Causes of the Wealth of Nations*. London: Penguin.

Tooker, L. and Clarke, C. (2018) 'Experiments in Relational Finance: Harnessing the Social in Everyday Debt and Credit', *Theory, Culture and Society*, 35, 3: pp 57–76.

Tooze, A. (2018) *Crashed: How a Decade of Financial Crises Changed the World*. London: Allen Lane.

Urry, J. (2011) *Climate Change and Society*. Cambridge: Polity.

Van Der Zwan, N. (2019) 'Making Sense of Financialization', *Socio-Economic Review*, 12, 1: pp 99–129.

Vigna, P. and Casey, M.J. (2018) *Cryptocurrency: How Bitcoin and Digital Money are Challenging the Global Economic Order*. London: Vintage.

Walby, S. (2013) 'Finance versus Democracy? Theorizing Finance in Society', *Work, Employment and Society*, 27, 3: pp 489–507.

Walby, S. (2015) *Crisis*. Cambridge: Polity.

Weber, M. [1922] (2019) *Economy and Society*. Cambridge, MA: Harvard University Press.

Weber, M. [1964] (1971) 'Religious Rejections of the World and their Directions', in H.H. Gerth and C.W. Mills (eds) *From Max Weber: Essays in Sociology*. New York: Oxford University Press, p 331.

Weiner, A.B. (1992) *Inalienable Possessions: The Paradox of Keeping-While Giving*. California: University of California Press.

Wittgenstein, L. [1921] (1981) *Tractatus Logico-Philosophicus*, trans C.K. Ogden. London: Taylor & Francis Ltd.

Wolf, M. (2020) 'Democracy will Fail if We don't Think as Citizens', *Financial Times*, 6 July, https://www.ft.com/content/36abf9a6-b838-4ca2-ba35-2836bd0b62e2, accessed 9 March 2021.

Wright, K. (2021) *Community Resilience: A Critical Perspective*. London: Routledge.

Zelizer, V.A. (1994) *The Social Meaning of Money: Pin Money, Paychecks, Poor Relief, and Other Currencies*. New York: Basic Books.

Zelizer, V.A. (2005) 'Circuits within Capitalism', in V. Nee and R. Swedberg (eds) *The Economic Sociology of Capitalism*. Princeton: Princeton University Press, pp 289–322.

Zelizer, V.A. (2012) 'How I Became a Relational Economic Sociologist and What Does That Mean?', *Politics and Society*, 20, 4: pp 145–74.

Index

Lightning Source UK Ltd.
Milton Keynes UK
UKHW051711061121
393341UK00006B/50